CAM

The Mount

A PRACTICAL GUIDE AND HANDBOOK

A.J. Drake

Third Edition 1990

CONTENTS

ISBN 0 9509580 2-6   May 1990.

PREFACE TO THIRD EDITION

Regrettably it is two years since the second edition sold out and it has taken much longer than expected to find the time for the necessary revision work and to take an adequate cover picture. It has been found desirable to amend 84 out of the 96 pages and once more I am very indebted to Joan Kelland for retyping many of the pages. Joan has also battled with the accommodation list which has proved to be a continuous task. With inflation still rising it has been decided to put the year to which prices given were relevant. At the time of writing the imposition of the standard business rate on bed and breakfast establishments was casting a shadow over the future of overnight accommodation and could mean closure of many of the addresses.

It is pertinent to ask whether the prospect of designation of the Cambrian Way as a national route has advanced since the last edition in 1985. The Countryside Commission has decided to create further long distance routes, now called National Trails, and also to tackle erosion problems on existing trails. In considering possible future national trails in Wales it must have cogitated on the project it supported for fourteen years before abandonment in 1982. The considerable uplift to the profile of country walking and the increasing consciousness of the value to the Welsh economy of tourism and farm diversification might well have worked in Cambrian Way's favour but the Commission clearly thought it was still too much of a "hot potato" and went for the easier option of Glyndwr's Way.

Meanwhile the route in this book is there for the connoisseur of mountain walking to follow - a Welsh coast to coast route over the highest, wildest and most attractive parts of Wales. There is much to be said for an unofficial written-up route which can reasonably use any rights of way or old established mountain top routes. The opposition of the farmers has been grossly exaggerated, as evidenced by the absence of disputes since the first route sheets were issued seventeen years ago. Provided walkers keep to the route, shut gates and generally respect the life and work of those whose land they cross, they will find the traditional Welsh "welcome in the hillsides". There are of course problems on any route and these have been taken up by the author who continues to monitor the route and put up and maintain waymarking, stiles, etc., on several stretches. An unofficial route means that changes to it can easily be made, where desirable, and several of these are incorporated in this edition, notably at Myddfai and between the Rheidol valley and Ystumtuen.

Prospective walkers on the Cambrian Way should not be deterred by the national survey of 1988 which suggested that a two mile walk in Wales, chosen at random from an Ordnance Survey map, had only a 16% chance of being possible, due to obstructions and other problems. Cambrian Way walkers will find few problems provided they are good map readers but deviation from the prescribed route onto other rights of way may well be troublesome.

THE MOUNTAIN CONNOISSEUR'S WALK

The Cambrian Way is a mountain walking route from Cardiff to Conwy traversing much of the highest, wildest and most scenically beautiful parts of Wales. It was originally conceived as a long distance path to be created under the National Parks & Access to the Countryside Act 1949, but following much opposition the Countryside Commission abandoned the scheme for its creation in 1982. The Way described in this guidebook is basically the route originally proposed by the Cambrian Way Committee in 1971, with some modifications to make greater use of existing public rights of way. Where the public does not have a legal or permissive right to go the Way is across mountain and moorland on routes where there has been de facto access for many years.

The Cambrian Way is designed for the connoisseur of mountain walking. It is not intended to appeal to the "beeliner" and those of the John o' Groats to Land's End mentality. It is for those who like to follow a well tried route, where the quality of the scenery has been the first consideration in planning. The Cambrian Way should be walked only for the pleasure and achievement it brings to the individual. It is not for the masochists who need to be spurred on by sponsorship.

At 274 miles (440Km) the length of the Cambrian Way is 24 miles more than the Pennine Way. A possible schedule making maximum use of youth hostels would be 293 miles. The ascent involved is 61,540 feet (18,779 metres) which is nearly double that of the Pennine Way. This greater ascent must be very seriously taken into account not only as to the length of time required, but also as to whether the Way should be attempted at all, especially if backpacking. With the average time taken for the Pennine Way being about nineteen days, the Cambrian Way is likely to need at least three days more. It is much more of a mountaineering expedition than the Pennine Way and is more of a high level route than the West Highland Way. 64% of the route is at over 800 feet (240 metres) above sea level. 20% is over 2,000 feet (610m) and 2½% is over 3,000 feet (915m).

A Countryside Commission survey of 1972 identified two factors above all others as to why people walked the Pennine Way. These were the scenery and the challenge. The Cambrian Way has both scenery and challenge in abundance.

Almost all of Wales can be said to be attractive but those parts designated as national parks have been selected because they are extensive tracts of country where their natural beauty calls for preservation and enhancement for the purpose of promoting their enjoyment by the public. 60% of the Cambrian Way is through the national parks of Snowdonia and the Brecon Beacons. A further 20% in central Wales is through what the Countryside Commission considered worthy of national park status but which the Secretary of State for Wales rejected as such in 1973. Even the remaining 20% is mostly through pleasant rolling country. Little industrialisation is seen and only one motorway is crossed. The biggest eyesore is Trawsfynydd nuclear power station.

The challenge is to find the physical and mental stamina to walk the continuous route. The Cambrian Way should not be the first long distance walk to be undertaken. Shorter, less arduous, ways should be tried first. Additional attributes are required on Cambrian Way. Wind and rain at higher altitudes can be quite destructive and demoralising. Waterproof clothing is absolutely essential and walkers should be warned of the really lethal effect of hypothermia, caused by the combination of a wet body and the cold conditions frequently experienced in mountains. Although some parts of the Way are on popular routes, most of it is unfrequented and where the way is undefined on the ground, and is unwaymarked. The additional height means that much of the time will be in cloud where navigation is bound to be difficult. Ability to use a compass is essential but more important is being able to read maps and particularly to interpret contours. The maps in this guidebook are designed so that they provide complete navigation requirements together with the 1:50,000 Landranger maps of the Ordnance Survey. The size of the guide is just less than the folded size of the Landranger maps to facilitate either carrying in a long hip pocket of one's walking breeches or, mounted in the open position, back to back with two side by side segments of the O.S. map in a map case or transparent plastic bag.

The routes described are not the result of just walking over the ground once and writing it up. Much surveying of possible routes was carried out by members of the Cambrian Way Committee, and the author must have spent over 200 days in surveys. The legal status of the route traversed has been carefully checked and visits have been made to all the county councils involved to view public path definitive maps, road records and commons registers. A few obstruction problems have been reported to the highway authorities. The original proposals assumed that new rights of way would be created following approval of the route by the Secretary of State for Wales. Surprisingly the greater use of rights of way has only resulted in an increase of six miles (2%) over the length proposed in 1971. As will be seen in the analysis on a later page, 85% of the Way is where the public either has a right to go or where there is permissive use. The remaining 15% is over mountain and moorland where de facto access has been enjoyed for many years.

It must be stressed that there is no official recognition to the Cambrian Way, either by the Countryside Commission or any of the authorities. Whilst the Commission strongly supported the project until 1978, most of the county and district councils along the route and the two national park authorities were opposed to the concept. The farming unions were vociferous in their opposition. Hopefully the use of the Way resulting from this guide will prove that the opposition was unjustified and that it will become accepted as has Wainwright's popular Coast to Coast walk across northern England.

Most of the well known summits of Wales are included, with Snowdon the highest point in England and Wales as a fitting climax. Some lesser known summits are visited but some of the well known ones are omitted. Notable amongst these are the Arans, not omitted because of the recent access restrictions, but because a route over the Arans does not fit in conveniently with the more interesting traverse of Cader Idris and the Rhinogs. The route is not always on the tops and sometimes deliberately follows a valley where the valley is particularly attractive. Thus the wild Doethie valley is followed for several miles and descent is made at Devil's Bridge to the gorge of the Rheiddol. Wales has many attractive woodlands of traditional hardwoods and several of these are visited.

Planning overnight accommodation is the biggest headache for most who walk long distance paths. The backpacker has fewer problems but must still find a site where his night's stay will not cause offence. The youth hostel chain is already more complete than it was on the Pennine Way when that path was opened, but immediate use resulting from this guide is necessary to stop more hostels being closed. Users of bed and breakfast houses will find a true "welcome in the hillside" from the comprehensive list in this guide, supplemented with cafes, pubs that do snacks and village shop/post offices.

THE HISTORY OF THE CAMBRIAN WAY

My first involvement in long distance path planning was in the early 1950s when the Ramblers Association in Gloucestershire worked out a route for the Cotswold Way. Later, amendments to the designated route for the Offa's Dyke path were negotiated in the Wye Valley. Between 1957 and 1960 I was involved in the planning of a serial walk along the Dyke path for the combined Gloucestershire rambling clubs. These were very popular and the cry was "What can we do next?" I did some preliminary planning for a route from Gloucester to Snowdon via the Black Mountains, Brecon Beacons and Plynlimon. The enormous attraction of this mostly mountain route was apparent, but the ramblers did not take it up. It was not until 1967 that it occurred to me to wonder why no one had proposed a long distance route over the principal mountains of Wales. Soundings in R.A. and Y.H.A. circles in Wales brought an immediate and enthusiastic response. S.Wales Area of the R.A. and S.Wales Region of the Y.H.A. each put up motions to their respective national councils in March 1968 calling for the creation of a Cambrian Way Long Distance Footpath.

The Cambrian Way Committee. Roger Brickell, the South Wales R.A. secretary at that time, convened a meeting at Kington Youth Hostel on June 23rd 1968, at which a Cambrian Way Committee was formed with myself as chairman and Roger as secretary. A predominantly high level mountain route was to be surveyed and various organisations undertook sections by counties. The south part was divided between the R.A., Y.H.A., the Brecon Beacons Voluntary Wardens Association and Pontypool Group of the R.A. In the north the British Mountaineering Council was to be offered the Caernarvonshire section but turned out to be hostile to the whole concept. Subsequently the R.A. and Y.H.A. based on Liverpool, joined forces, led by Bill Hall and Brian Steventon respectively, and surveyed all the northern half.

The survey methods varied considerably. In the south some of the committee, notably Bob Rowson and Keith Mascetti were already knowledgeable of their area. Denis Veasey, David Robinson and Don Sutor made surveys in the lesser known Elenydd and concluded that the western side of that wild area had fewer forestry problems. The Liverpool ramblers and hostellers had different methods and descended on their allotted area by coach and dispersed into several survey groups. Although I had visited much of Wales, particularly on meets of the Gloucestershire Mountaineering Club, my roving commission on all sections took me to many delightful parts of Wales I might never have gone to.

My first proposal was for a route from Capel-y-ffin to Snowdon but this soon got extended in both directions. Capel-y-ffin was clearly no equivalent of Edale but proposals to start a little further south at Abergavenny did not satisfy the South Wales members of the committee, who devised a route from Cardiff skirting the coalfield. At the north end the natural extension was to the North Wales coast and soon the attraction of the long ridge of the Carneddau and the idea of a castle to castle route clinched Conwy as the northern terminal.

At the subsequent three meetings of the committee the difficulty of arriving at a consensus view increased and there was a temptation to suggest alternatives because of disagreement. However, certain alternatives were agreed upon for safety reasons, such as a lower level alternative to the Rhinog ridgeline, and the Pyg Track or Crib Goch on Snowdon.

One alternative never properly resolved was whether to go north from Plynlimon to Cader Idris via Machynlleth or the longer way via Dylife, Dinas Mawddwy and Maesglasau. (See later in the guide for the main arguments.) There was considerable discussion over the Black Mountains, partly as to whether to include them, and, if so, where to cross over to the Brecon Beacons. I never liked the variation proposed via Mynydd Llangorse and Talybont, because it omitted the very fine Pen Allt Mawr ridge, and the Llangattock cave area. The Brecon Park wardens advocated use of the Brecon & Usk canal towpath from

Llangattock and Talybont but I could never see keen mountain walkers wanting to walk nine miles of towpath however attractive.

The 1971 Proposals. On July 10th 1971, after the ceremony at Knighton declaring the Offa's Dyke Path officially open, I handed John Cripps, chairman of the Countryside Commission, a set of maps giving the Cambrian Way Committee's proposed route for Cambrian Way. In November that year the Interim Report was produced and this lamentably was the only information on the Cambrian Way that I found time to produce until the first edition of this guidebook in 1984. Many hundreds of a scruffy 34 page duplicated report were sold to would be walkers until most of the stencils wore out.

The Countryside Commission has the responsibility for making recommendations to the Secretaries of State for the Environment or for Wales for the creation of long distance paths, under provisions of the National Parks & Access to the Countryside Act, 1949. Routes approved by the Secretary of State become the responsibility of the local authorities to create with 100% grant from national funds. New rights of way can be created by agreement or compulsorily by creation order.

The Commission from the beginning made encouraging noises and first mentioned the Cambrian Way in its annual report for 1968. The Interim Report was well received but it was made clear that restricted resources would dictate only limited commitment to the proposals. This proved to be a considerable understatement, such that the Commission's next four annual reports only indicated that the route was "under consideration". It sought to get reactions from the likely user organisations before approaching local authority and landowning interests. The Committee for Wales of the Countryside Commission was enthusiastic both under the chairmanship of Dr. Margaret Davies and later of Trevor Lewis and James Kegie.

In April 1976 the Commission approved the Cambrian Way project in principle and in September 1977 started official consultations on the basis of a map showing both the Cambrian Way Committee's route and the Commission's preferred route which differed in many respects. All the principal summits in Snowdonia were omitted. The route was to go over the Arans and the Arenigs instead of the Rhinogs and Cader Idris. The crossover from Black Mountains to Brecon Beacons was to be via Mynydd Llangorse.

Following opposition from many quarters, the Commission issued another line in January 1980 called a Consultation Route. This time the Cambrian Way Committee's route was not shown on the map, though the new route was closer to it than the 1977 line. Snowdon was included but still not the ridge of the Carneddau. Cader Idris was included and a route to the seaward side of the Rhinogs instead of a route over the Arans, where in the meantime an access row had blown up. The Black Mountains were omitted altogether following pressure from the national park authority. There had been much criticism of lack of consultation by the Commission, so to meet this it had decided to appoint field officers to meet landowners and other authorities.

The first field officer, John Tetlow, a lecturer of the Department of Town Planning at the University of Wales, was appointed for a year and asked to report on the southern section up to Llandovery. He started off full of enthusiasm and the right ideas but when confronted with the opposition of commoners' committees and the national park authority, came up with some extraordinary compromises. Neither Pen y Fan nor the Carmarthen Van summits were to be part of the route, Pen y Fan because of erosion problems on the obvious route, and the Vans because the commoners would only agree to a route creeping round the base of the common and through conifer woods. The Cnewr Estate would not agree to any access during its lambing period (April 15th to May 10th) and the Countryside Commission was not prepared to have a long distance path with such a limitation.

After years of support for the project and considerable determination to see Cambrian Way come to fruition, the Countryside Commission suddenly caved in and, with regret, abandoned it in January 1982. It concluded that there was continuing and widespread opposition to the proposed route, even when alternatives were considered. It was one of the earliest major decisions of the Commission following the appointment of Derek (now Sir Derek) Barber as its new chairman. The decision was seen as an act of appeasement to the Welsh farmers in the hope of more cooperation on other countryside issues.

The second field officer, Donald Hoare, of Cwmystwyth, a former principal of an outdoor pursuits centre in Wales, fared better than John Tetlow and had found general acceptance of the Cambrian Way proposals in the central section up to the time of the termination of his appointment when the main project was abandoned. The Commission never got round to appointing a field officer for the northern section. Who knows what ghastly compromises he might have been forced into in the Snowdonia National Park?

The Recreational Organisations

The Ramblers Association has consistently supported the Cambrian Way project. Its National Executive Committee approved the principle of a Cambrian Way following a special meeting, which I attended, in July 1972 but agreed that any guide on the subject should stress that it was a mountain route. It was proposed that the title should be "The Cambrian Mountain Way".

The Youth Hostels Association likewise consistently supported the idea of a high level route with low level alternatives. It looked forward to an exciting new outlet for the energies of young travellers.

The British Mountaineering Council's North Wales Committee was bitterly opposed to the idea of a Cambrian Way and in particular to it going over the Rhinogs. At a meeting in February 1972, at which the author was representing the Gloucestershire Mountaineering Club, only the London Mountaineering Club representative gave support. The B.M.C.'s South-west and Southern Committee, covering South Wales, decided in favour so that the matter was called in nationally. I attended a meeting of the Committee of Management in October 1972 and after an hour and a half's debate Cambrian Way was approved by 11 votes to 4. Subsequently however the B.M.C. Safety Committee secured a reversal of the decision on safety grounds, and thought that designation would "encourage peak baggers and merit badge enthusiasts into difficult and remote areas". The North Wales Committee was asked to work out an alternative to the Rhinogs and it was their route over the relatively dull Arenig Fawr and moorland to the south-east of Ffestiniog that appeared as the Countryside Commission's preferred route in 1977.

The County Councils and the National Parks

Numerically the county councils were equally divided as to the merits of a Cambrian Way, Gwent, South Glamorgan and Mid Glamorgan being in favour with Dyfed, Gwynedd and Powys against. Those against however controlled 87% of the proposed route.

Both the national park authorities opposed the Cambrian Way. Brecon Beacons National Park claimed that the route proposed was neither logical nor in keeping with the policies of the national park plan. That plan defined the Carmarthen Vans as a remote and vulnerable area where additional recreation activity would not be encouraged by the provision of further facilities. The use of two further ridges of the Black Mountains for a long distance path was said to be difficult to accept and support. Despite the 100% grants available for long distance paths it was argued that concentration of limited resources on long distance paths reduced the amount of work carried out on the path network generally. It was pointed out that the cost of erosion work in the Brecon Beacons was falling entirely on the national park and the National Trust, but no mention was made that 100% grant could be available if the erosion was on an official long distance route.

The opposition continues and the national park committee even went to the length of passing a resolution in 1986 to ban the sale of this book from its bookshop at the Mountain Centre near Brecon.

Snowdonia National Park in its national park plan (1977) said "The National Park Authority is not convinced of the desirability of the proposed Cambrian Way long distance footpath. In particular they are opposed to the suggested route linking most of the principal summits of Snowdonia. The Authority will therefore seek further discussions on the topic with the Countryside Commission and other interested bodies." They certainly had discussions with the Commission but not with the R.A. or Y.H.A.

The Farming Interests

Both the National Farmers Union and the Farmers Union of Wales were vociferous in their opposition to Cambrian Way and used their powerful lobby to influence the local authorities and park committees. The Country Landowners Association was apparently not opposed to the project.

THE INSTANT CAMBRIAN WAY

The arguments raged furiously from 1968 to 1982 as to whether a Cambrian Way was desirable and if so where it should go. If the project had not been abandoned, the arguments would probably have gone on for decades and the end result, if any, would at best have been a set of miserable compromises.

It was becoming apparent, even before abandonment, that if the compromises being considered were adopted, there would have arisen the anomalous situation of Cambrian Way walkers watching others go the obvious well established ways while they were plodding round the edges of commons and missing the tops. Guidebooks would have appeared advocating different routes to the official line and the whole concept of long distance paths would have fallen into disrepute.

Following abandonment there was a freedom to choose any way over which the public has a right of way or access, or where there is permissive use. On commons and other open country it is reasonable to describe well used routes - there would have been no books on mountain walks in Wales if rights of way only had to be followed.

With hindsight it is perhaps a pity I did not produce a guidebook during the mid 70s but the need not to prejudice possible new rights of way was felt to be paramount. After abandonment much further survey was carried out to make more use of existing rights of way. In the event I was "pipped at the post" by Richard Sale, whose "A Cambrian Way" was published in February 1984. Constables had commissioned Richard to write a book which was not to be published until the route became official. After abandonment they decided to go ahead but to avoid certain controversial areas. Subtitled "A personal guide to an unofficial route", the book is not a practical guide and handbook as this book sets out to be, but has 270 pages packed with fascinating reading, mostly historical, and which makes excellent reading after a day on the Cambrian Way. Richard and I had several meetings to coordinate routes but we agreed to differ on some. Richard's book was published too early to take advantage of the purchase of part of Fforest Fawr by Brecon Beacons National Park and the permissive arrangements for the Cnewr estate had not been announced. Although Richard uses the Machynlleth variant from Plynlimon, he did write up the Dinas Mawddwy route as an alternative, but Constables thought the book was long enough. Hopefully others will write books on other aspects of the Cambrian Way such as the industrial archaeology, geology and bird life.

How can it be that the Cambrian Way, officially abandoned after much opposition, suddenly came into existence at the behest of

Messrs. Drake and Sale? Is it irresponsible to take advantage of the
right of any citizen to suggest to others where they may walk? Some
books have undoubtedly caused embarrassment where insufficient research
has been carried out as to rights of way and as to possible impacts on
wildlife and erosion problems. The public status of the routes in this
guidebook has been the subject of all reasonable checks and has been
made by one who has a background of 40 years experience in handling
rights of way problems. The sections of the route over de facto
access land on rural commons (10%) and other mountain and moorland
(4%) have been carefully chosen to be along well established routes
where even the most law abiding walker would not feel it necessary to
try to ascertain who the owner was and to ask permission to use.

The following pages detail how the aspects that caused opposition
have been considered and taken into account in evolving the routes in
this guide. Meanwhile it is pertinent to ask how different the walker
will find the route compared with the official long distance paths.

Some sections are already popular routes and are maintained to a
reasonable standard, but many sections, including some in the national
parks, are poorly maintained or not at all, so walkers must take things
as they find them. One of the joys of Cambrian Way is that on many of
the higher level sections the way is undefined on the ground. Some of
these sections may develop a defined path in time but much will still be
wild and give that sense of remoteness that so many seek and do not
find on our long distance paths.

The main difference that long distance path addicts will find is that
there is little signposting and even less waymarking than one may be
accustomed to. Stiles and gates are nearly all of a low standard.
These aspects are elaborated on below. A few obstructions have been
found and reported to the county councils and mostly cleared by the
time of writing. Some diversions are desirable to provide a better
route, often to avoid farmyards, and in some cases to legalise diversions
which are already followed. Already one diversion order has become
operative, in Forestry Commission land north of Dylife, in anticipation
of use arising from this guide.

There are about 90 stiles and 165 gates on the main route - a fair
number but compared to the Offa's Dyke Path, with its 450 stiles and
125 gates (in only 176 miles), Cambrian Way is clearly less of a steeple-
chase. The difference reflects how different the terrain and land use
is, with so much more open country. However, that said, be warned
about the gates. Very few Welsh gates are properly hung. The majority
are held up at one or both ends with binder twine and sometimes with
barbed wire. Getting over these gates can be a greater hazard than
many more expected dangers. Maintenance of stiles and gates is the
responsibility of whoever maintains the fence, wall or hedge. A grant
of at least 25% of the cost is available but seldom claimed as it is just
not worth the bother. One might expect gates in regular use to be
reasonably well maintained but little used gates, and more particularly
stiles, are way down most farmers' priority list for attention. There is
little incentive to improve stiles and gates for the benefit of the public
and often a distinct inclination to discourage passage by those whose
dogs may chase their sheep. Many counties make use of unemployed
persons, mobilised into M.S.C. funded teams, to install stiles and gates,
and hopefully this will be arranged on the Cambrian Way route.

As with maintenance, so also the extent of signposting and waymarking is patchy. More waymarking is desirable to avoid trespass in
the lower sections, in the interests of both walker and farmer. I hope
to carry out a certain amount of waymarking myself, with the permission
of the farmers concerned, using the Countryside Commission system of
yellow painted arrows for footpaths and blue for bridleways. This is
also a task which can be carried out by M.S.C. path teams. On the
open mountains waymarking is much less acceptable and appropriate.
Cairns are the natural and traditional method, though less efficient than
arrows, but should be used sparingly, such as at particular descent
points like the top of the Zig Zags on Snowdon.

MEETING THE OPPOSITION

This section reviews the main reasons for opposition to the
designation of the Cambrian Way as an official long distance path
and shows how these aspects have been taken into account in planning
the routes in this guide.

Erosion

It is only in recent years that erosion has been taken seriously.
The enormous increase in mountain walking in the last forty years has
caused the breaking up of the surface of many popular routes. While
natural erosion is accepted as a fact of life erosion that is man made
offends. Attitudes to erosion are now less hysterical than they were
when Cambrian Way was first advocated and research and experiment has
shown that much erosion can be coped with or prevented. Other more
difficult problems remain and seem insoluble. One is inclined to feel that
if we can land men on the moon then surely something can be done
about erosion. It should not be necessary to discourage access to mountains because what amounts to a very small area is wearing away offen-
sively and because some of such problems defy solution. Like the
Cambrian Way itself, erosion is a challenge to be tackled and not something that is used as an excuse to discourage worth while activities.

A sense of proportion is necessary in considering erosion. A few
thousand extra walkers going up Snowdon will make little difference when
the numbers using the paths there run into millions over the years.
Where excessive numbers have caused erosion remedial action appropriate to the situation is a justifiable expense. The public had the
Snowdon paths on the cheap in the past, but under the management
scheme of recent years sterling work has been done by both volunteers
and paid staff and the problem is now under control.

Much consideration has been given to erosion problems in planning
the Cambrian Way route in this guide. As the Cambrian Way is envisaged
as a south to north route and since most erosion is caused in descent,
(and more particularly by those who run down), many eroded spots
which are taken in ascent are not likely to be further eroded by Cambrian Way traffic. Where the eroded ascent is itself a hazard, such as
Penyrole-wen, an alternative, albeit longer, ascent has been recommended. Some eroded descents have been avoided such as the north face
of Blorenge and the descent from Glyder Fawr to Llyn Cwn and Cwm
Idwal.

One type of erosion which is never likely to be a serious problem
on the Cambrian Way, but which has often been quoted against it, is
the traverse of peat bogs of the kind which cause such problems on the
Pennine Way. No really satisfactory solution seems to have been found
to the ever widening detours required to get round the bogs, but fortunately there is little similar terrain on the Cambrian Way. Horse riding
has been the main cause of erosion on the Black Mountains but it would
be most unfair to deny walkers the superb mountain walking there because horse riding has not been adequately brought under control.

Many sections are on broad ridges where, if use had been spread
evenly, no breaking up of the grass cover would have occurred. Inevitably however people tend to follow where a path becomes visible,
and if used to excess erosion occurs. Our Mountain Connoisseur must
use discretion and decide whether to walk well away from the worn path
or whether using the path will cause no more erosion. Generally one
can serve the cause better by keeping to one side, but not immediately
on the edge of the path - that's the next bit to go.

The relative contribution of Cambrian Way walkers to erosion at
already eroded sites will be small but care has had to be taken in
planning to avoid routes where only a relatively little usage could cause
a nasty gash in the mountainside. For this reason steep descents have
been avoided such as the new permissive way off Fan Gihirych on the
Cnewr Estate.

The ghastly upper section of the Watkin Path was included in the Countryside Commission's 1980 consultative route yet this part of the Snowdon Horseshoe is quite unnecessary if approaching Snowdon from the south-east. The much nicer Allt Maenderyn ridge leading to Bwlch Main is also showing some signs of having appeared in guide books, but it is a wide stony ridge which is unlikely to provide serious problems and will not wear away for a few million years yet.

An unsolved problem is the south-east ridge of Pen y Fan which is a much softer slope. Any solution is likely to look artificial. Probably large stone steps are the answer but unfortunately they are not so readily available as they were for repair of the Snowdon paths.

The Farmers

I am sure the farmers were needlessly alarmed about the Cambrian Way. They tend to see any proposals for more public access as meaning more sheep worried and killed by dogs, more gates left open, more walls and fences climbed over and more vandalism generally. Each farmer you meet has some horrific tale to tell. One bad incident is inclined to sour a farmer for ever against the public.

Some farmers are very possessive, while others have a greater sense of holding the land in trust and are willing to share use with those who get a pleasure from walking the mountains. Most Welsh farmers are friendly and enjoy a chat if they are not too busy. In all my walks planning the Cambrian Way I have only once been challenged by a farmer and that was on a right of way.

The farmers are a very powerful lobby in the rural counties of Wales. They can attend daytime meetings of county and district councils and national park committees, and used their muscle to oppose Cambrian Way. One wonders if those opposing the project had any idea of the satisfaction that many people derive from following a long continuous route on foot. For certain few, if any, had walked a long distance path - and that goes for most other opponents.

Other long distance paths were said to give farmers trouble, including Offa's Dyke, yet Offa's Dyke Association seldom hears of any problems. It hears much more from farmers wanting to be put on the bed and breakfast list. There are said to be 1250 farms providing accommodation and meals in Wales. Farm tourism means a lot to the economy of the uplands, and with farm subsidies now very much being questioned a second form of income, from path walkers, should be more than welcome.

I am sure that Cambrian Way walkers will be better behaved than the average car tourist and holiday maker, if only because there will be little time to get up to mischief as there is an objective to be reached each day. In any case, those who have the strength of character to embark on an expedition such as the Cambrian Way are most unlikely to come from the strata of to-day's society that is involved in petty crime and vandalism. There are however "black sheep in every family" and some of the problems farmers suffer from are due to sheer ignorance or incompetence, so the following particular aspects of countryside behaviour are mentioned specifically.

Dogs. Whatever you do don't take a dog with you on the Cambrian Way. Dogs are the cause of more antagonism from farmers than any other cause. It is now an offence to walk with a dog in a field of sheep unless the dog is on a lead or "under close control" (maximum fine £400). A farmer can shoot a dog worrying, or about to worry, livestock. Even the most placid of dogs can go berserk on seeing sheep and it is claimed that thousands of sheep are killed by dogs every year. Even if your dog is well behaved, you will be regarded with great suspicion by farmers. As far as I am concerned, no one who has had a dog with them will qualify for having walked the Cambrian Way.

Gates. A gate left open can cause the most awful problems. I heard of one farmer who brought several hundred sheep down to the valley the day before contractors' vans were to collect them. Someone left a gate open and not only did the vans go away empty, but the sheep got onto another farm and it took days to sort out the chaos. Remember farmers should not lock gates on a bridleway, so locking may not be the answer. Sometimes you find gates open. I do not entirely subscribe to the Country Code which tells you to shut all gates. You may be depriving animals of access to water. It is better to leave them as you find them, but if in doubt - shut. Leaders of parties should ask someone with them at the front to stay with the gate until the party is through, whether it has to be closed or not.

Rights of Way. Make certain that your map reading is impeccable so that you can keep to the rights of way across farmland. Use both the Ordnance Survey maps and the maps in this guide and consult them frequently. Good map reading will be much more required than on, say, the Pennine Way. Avoid getting into the situation where you have to trespass to get back on course. Ensure that all members of a party have the necessary maps and can map read. Contour map reading is important, particularly at higher levels, and experience with this aspect may prove vital in cloud conditions.

Many farmers do not know where their rights of way are or may try to persuade you to go another way. If your right of passage is denied on what you believe to be a public right of way, use due discretion as to insisting on your rights. It is important to report such incidents to the county council and the Ramblers Association.

Nature Conservation

It speaks well for the defences built up by the nature conservation movement that the routing for the Cambrian Way was questioned in several places on conservation grounds. One had, however, to resist the almost automatic reaction of "You can't go that way - that's a nature reserve". One had to ask (a) what was it that was being conserved at that site, (b) what effect would Cambrian Way usage have on it, and (c) would that effect really matter? Generally the more knowledgeable the conservationist the more reasonable the answers received, and frequently it was clear that there was no real problem. One also concluded that the nature conservationists were often their own worst enemies in that they cannot keep secrets as to locations of rare species. Just as we were being told that a certain national nature reserve should be avoided, a radio broadcast was saying that this was the only place in the world that a certain tree grew. Walkers on the Cambrian Way are highly unlikely to be interested in identifying rare trees and digging them up. Nevertheless, I am not saying in this guide where that tree grows.

The kite is not the only rare bird in Wales but was the only one mentioned as likely to be affected by the Cambrian Way, particularly in the Towy valley. This matter is covered more fully in the main text under "Rhandirmwyn". The effect in the nesting season of a few more walkers going up the Doethie valley will surely be very minimal.

Early in 1972 the Nature Conservancy offices at Bangor and Aberystwyth requested copies of the Cambrian Way Interim Report, which were sent with an offer to discuss any problems likely to arise on the routes concerned. In the autumn of that year, having heard nothing, I wrote to the Director of the Nature Conservancy asking for informal discussions. The reply, from the assistant director for Wales, was that discussions would be premature, so my attempts to become better informed were thwarted. No one can say I didn't try.

The Danger Aspects

It might be thought that one was proposing a walk over the highest peaks in the Alps to judge from some of the remarks passed about the dangers of the Cambrian Way. None of the summits traversed are technically difficult by the routes suggested for any normally healthy person, but of course any mountain can be a hazard in bad weather conditions, and the higher and steeper it is, the more the danger. Surely there is still scope for a spice of adventure in life. The critics point to the people who have to be rescued from the mountains because of ignorance of the basic requirements of equipment or because of foolhardiness in just not appreciating the hazards of venturing in the mountains. As with road safety, one can only go on plugging the need for care, rather than banning the pastime.

The attitude of many of the climbing fraternity was condescending to walkers to say the least. One statement made that particularly stuck in the gullet was that "paths should be laid out in areas of no interest to mountaineers". The attitude over use of the Rhinogs was near hysterical and akin to the sort of opposition Tom Stephenson had to his proposals to take the Pennine Way over Kinderscout. That wild moor was then forbidden territory. The northern Rhinogs provide a fantastic walk over rough and rocky ground, but in this case there is a public right of access to it, as it is Crown common. The national park authority would have the Rhinogs put in a glass case, labelled "Wilderness". Granted that such an area should not be developed for general tourist use but the one recreational use it is suitable for is a tough high level walk. If wilderness areas must be found, there are plenty of other parts of Wales that few want to go to which could qualify.

There was much pressure to work out a lower level alternative route, but really those who want such routes should follow other long distance paths and not try adulterating a natural high level route. The sort of compromises which were being proposed in the Brecon Beacons area just before abandonment were completely debasing the concept of a high level route. As a concession to mountain safety and as official long distance routes have to have specific routes designated, the Cambrian Way Committee put forward additional alternative routes for the Rhinogs, and for the Snowdon and Glyder areas, based on the precedent of official alternatives on the Pennine Way and Offa's Dyke. These have not been specified so precisely in this guide because there is much greater flexibility anyway with an unofficial route. Many alternatives are mentioned or are apparent from the Ordnance Survey maps.

RIGHTS OF WAY AND ACCESS

It is important that walkers on the Cambrian Way should be conscious both of their right to proceed and of their obligations to those who live and work on the land they traverse. Whatever their rights, as detailed in the paragraphs below, they should always regard their travel over the land as a privilege given and accepted by persons mostly long since departed, and only occasionally due to recent negotiations.

A high proportion (161½ miles = 59%) of the recommended routes are over public rights of way (also known as "highways"). There are varying degrees of public right of passage according to the status of the highway. If the way is a public footpath there is a right of way on foot. A bridleway has the additional right of riding or leading a horse or of riding a pedal cycle. "Roads used as public paths" may have vehicular rights of passage and "Byways open to all traffic" certainly have. These categories of highway are marked on the Ordnance Survey maps by different symbols, in red for the 1:50,000 scale and in green for the 1:25,000 Leisure and Pathfinder series. The O.S. gets its information from definitive maps of rights of way prepared by county councils and the existence of a path on the definitive map is conclusive evidence that it was a right of way at the relevant date of the map. Legal orders changing rights of way are usually notified to the O.S. but some did not get through such as the diversions in connection with the Traswfynydd power station and Llyn Stwlan.

Public roads are mostly shown in various colours on the O.S. maps according to status but there are many public roads that are uncoloured. These "white" roads are mostly untarred stony roads or green lanes and are indistinguishable on the maps from private roads. It is however usually safe to infer that a white road is public if public paths are shown as terminating on it. Cambrian Way follows several of these white roads, checks on their status having been made at county offices.

Rights of way have become established by prolonged usage with the acquiescence of the owner of the land, and must be on a defined route. Although many public paths exist over open country it is common for the way to be less defined. When the survey of rights of way was being conducted from which the definitive maps were derived uncertainty as to the line of paths across open land often led to them being marked only to the edge of the open country. This was not thought to matter as the facility to roam at large was never disputed. This can however present problems if right of access is disputed. In English law one cannot establish a right to roam at large by continued usage with acquiescence of the owner, as one can with defined rights of way. There are however some categories of open country where the public has a legal right of access and this has considerable relevance to the Cambrian Way.

Urban Commons

Under the Law of Property Act 1925 the public acquired a right of access for "air and exercise" to commons that at the time were administered by borough or urban district councils. At the south end of Cambrian Way this includes Mynydd Machen and a long line of commons from Twmbarlwm, near Newport, to just south of the Blorenge near Abergavenny. At the north end Tal y Fan, Conwy Mountain and the exciting traverse path leading to the Sychnant Pass are on commons in former urban districts. 11½ miles of the Way are over non-definitive routes on urban commons.

Crown commons

Under the same act owners of common land were able to make a deed of declaration which gave the public the same rights of access over commons in former rural districts. In 1932 this procedure was adopted by the Crown Commissioners for its extensive commons in the rural districts of Wales (though not for England). Thus sections of the Cambrian Way, amounting to 11 miles, run over public access crown commons, including the northern parts of the Carneddau, Plynlimon, the northern Rhinogs, Moelwyn Mawr, Domen Milwyn and Teifi Pools.

The Birmingham Clauses

The route passes over the fringe of the gathering grounds of the Elan Valley reservoirs which are covered by the famous "Birmingham Clauses" which give "the public a privilege at all times to enjoy air, exercise and recreation".

Difference between Rights of Way and Access

A right of way is a greater right over its width than a right of access. With a right of way the highway authority has a duty to maintain and to keep it free from obstruction. No such duty applies over the area of land to which the public may have access so that one cannot expect bridges everywhere over streams or the clearing of gorse and bracken.

National Trust Land

Several sections of Cambrian Way traverse National Trust land which is open to the public. The longest stretch of non-definitive route on National Trust land is the high parts of the Carneddau from Ogwen to Drum. Other sections are on Sugar Loaf, Pen y Fan, and the Glyders - total 10 miles.

National Park Authority Land

It cannot be too often stressed that land in national parks is generally privately owned and that national park status does not give the public any additional right of access. In recent years however the Brecon Beacons National Park Authority has itself acquired certain large tracts of common land in order to ensure public access. This applies to the eastern section of Fforest Fawr (Great Forest) (see page 35) and the west side of the Black Mountain (see page 43). In 1989 it entered into a management agreement with Welsh Water for the western part of Fforest Fawr (the east side of Black Mountain). This will safeguard public access on foot. These sections cover 12 miles (4½%) of the main Cambrian Way route.

Forestry Commission Land

The Commission allows general access on foot to its land subject to certain restrictions. Two sections of the Cambrian Way are on non-definitive paths by arrangement with the district officer concerned.

Cardiff

Cardiff City has no definitive map as yet but the route follows publically maintained paths and roads or is through public parks or council owned former canal towpath open to the public.

Rural Commons

Commons in areas administered before 1974 by rural district councils do not normally provide a legal right of access for the public, unless there is a Law of Property Act deed. In practice the facility to roam is virtually never disputed. The Countryside Commission supports the policy of the Ramblers Association and the Open Spaces Society in advocating legislation to give the public a legal right of access to all commons, albeit with reasonable restrictions and the rules of behaviour as recommended by the Royal Commission on Commons in 1958 and the Common Land Forum in 1986.

The longest stretch of rural common on the Cambrian Way is the Black Mountains section from Bal Mawr via the Tumpa, Waun Fach and Pen Allt Mawr to Table Mountain near Crickhowell. All this is very well known as a mountain walk. Another such section is Mynydd Llangynidr. On these commons there is "de facto" access and no one would dream of trying to find out who the owner was and asking permission to walk over them. Other large stretches of rural commons include Fforest Fawr and the Black Mountain, as referred to above.

Open Country Access Land

There remain a few sections on high ground that do not fall into any of the above categories but which are open country with de facto access, that is to say that so far as is known walkers are not denied access as long as they act in a reasonable manner - hopefully a situation that will long continue. None of these sections are at low level.

These sections are over land which comes within the definition of open country in Part V of the National Parks & Access to the Countryside Act 1949. Amongst the types of country in the definition are mountain and moorland. The Act did not give the public any right of access to open country but provided the means whereby local authorities could secure public access in cases where it was denied or agreed by the parties to be desirable. A public right of access can be obtained either by agreement or compulsorily by order. The Act provides for possible limitiations on access such as for periods of grouse shooting, and enables the payment of compensation for allowing access and the provision of a warden service.

Although several access agreements have been made in the Peak District few have so far been made in Wales. Agreements have sometimes been made for limited access without formal proceedings. Snowdonia National Park were under strong pressure to make an access agreement, or failing that an access order, for the Arans (mercifully never on the author's proposed route for Cambrian Way). The compromise arrived at was not an agreement under the National Parks Act and only provided for defined routes instead of access. Hopefully the aggravations which precipitated the denial of access on the Arans will not occur on the sections of Cambrian Way where there is no legal right of access. Much will depend on the good behaviour of Cambrian Way walkers.

Continued on page 18

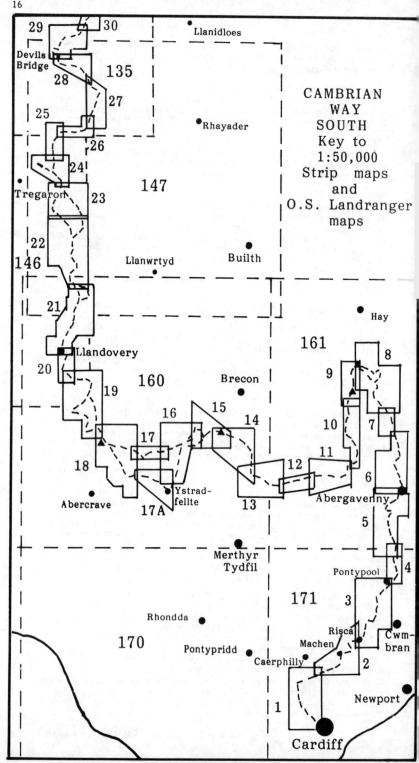

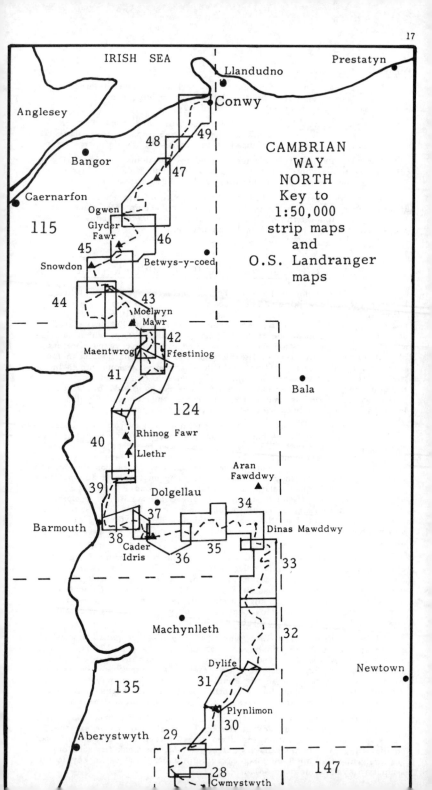

Other Non-Definitive Sections

New routes. In three instances waymarked paths are followed which have been negotiated by the National Park authorities. These may or may not be dedicated as rights of way.

Uncertain status routes. In two cases paths are followed which appear to be public but are not on the definitive maps or road plans. It may be that they should be claimed at the review of the definitive maps.

Courtesy Paths - this phrase, coined in Snowdonia, applies to certain negotiated routes such as the way from Pen-y-Pass to Glyder Fawr over open country in ownership of Mrs. Esme Kirby.

Unofficial Diversions. Frequently the route on the ground is different from the definitive route. A diversion should take place but meanwhile one follows the obvious route and if anyone complains the proper right of way will have to be opened up.

PLANNING TO WALK THE CAMBRIAN WAY

The main decision to be made is how one is to spend the nights in between the daily walking. The accommodation list in this guide gives addresses mostly of the Bed and Breakfast variety. Although youth hostels appear briefly in the geographical order of the list, a separate section gives details of the 20 hostels on or near the Way, which provide a more complete chain than Pennine Way had even many years after its official opening. In parts of the Elenydd and Snowdonia hostels in fact provide the only accommodation available. The most serious gap is in the centre of the Rhinogs following the lamentable closure of Gerthi Bluog hostel. Some other gaps are well covered by B.&B. but sections where accommodation is limited are the area to the north of Plynlimon and in the semi-industrialised valleys crossed near Newport.

The Cambrian Way is superb backpacking country provided the weather is kind, but Wales has an enormous rainfall in the mountains. However, the backpacker has greater freedom as to where to decide to stop and camp for the night. There are a few official camp sites en route and these are listed with the accommodation. It is most important that backpackers should get permission to camp on farmland and not take liberties that will upset relations with farmers who as a body fought vigorously against official designation of the Cambrian Way. It should be noted that there is no right to camp on common land and camping is specifically prohibited on National Trust land, water gathering grounds, and most other land to which the public has a right of access for air and exercise.

Those who are used to fell walking but not to carrying a big load over mountains should think twice before deciding to take camping equipment in case accommodation is not forthcoming. Cambrian Way has double the Pennine Way's ascent and is very wet under foot even in a dry summer. Wet feet and high loads are a sure recipe for blisters, not to mention problems of overbalancing on wet rocks, and possible ankle sprains miles from roads or habitation.

Don't make Cambrian Way your first long distance path, especially if you are backpacking and haven't carried camping gear before. Above all allow adequate time - at least three days more than for the Pennine Way - to allow for the extra ascent - and remember there is a high drop-out rate even on the Pennine Way. Cambrian Way is altogether a tougher proposition than other long distance paths in Britain and is through many remote areas with little or no public transport.

For further information on planning to walk the Cambrian Way turn to pages 78 to 96 at the back of the book. What now follows are the pages of general description and strip maps, placed centrally in the book so that they can, if desired, be extracted from the book for ease of reading while walking (see "Map carrying", page 81, also the key to the strip map symbols on page 96).

ROUTE DESCRIPTION AND STRIP MAPS

SOUTHERN SECTION

CARDIFF TO LLANDOVERY
Via the Black Mountains & Brecon Beacons

Distance 107   miles   Ascent 31163 feet

The southern section of the Cambrian Way is the longer of the three
sections into which the route naturally divides. Most of it is within the
Brecon Beacons and Black Mountains National Park which is entered
just north of Pontypool, at 26 miles from the start. These non-national
park miles are through the counties of South Glamorgan, Mid Glamorgan
and Gwent, which were the only counties not to oppose the concept of
the Cambrian Way. Much of the route through these counties may
receive 50% grant aid from the Countryside Commission as a recreational
route.

Although Cardiff may sound like an unpromising start for a mountain walk it is possible by starting at the Castle to step straight into
parkland and to follow a green belt between the built up area and the
River Taff for over three miles before meeting a small industrial area.
The M4 interchange crossing is horrific or fascinating according to
taste but then the towers of Castell Coch beckon and one follows
pleasant woodland and pastureland on the ridge between Cardiff and
Caerphilly before crossing the ends of the famous mining valleys of
Rhymney and Ebbw.

The coalfield itself is by-passed to the south and east. The
scenery in general is acceptable for a long distance path but in terms
of the Cambrian Way is only a foretaste of better things to come.

Although the walk is rewarding it is not through a tourist area.
It crosses industrial valleys where accommodation is scarce at present.
Risca is about half way but even 15-mile-a-day walkers would be ad-
vised to break themselves in by doing this stretch in 2½ to 3 days.

Cardiff to Tongwynlais   5.4 miles   125 feet of ascent   (maps 1 & 1A)

As already explained under "Maps" (page 80) it is assumed that
the walker has the 1:50,000 Ordnance Survey maps in addition to this
guide. The description is not a stile by stile account and only serves
to supplement the maps with useful information.

The first problem is that the gates to Cathays Park at the side of
Cardiff Castle are not open until after early starters will have departed.
However the west bank route through Sophia Gardens is almost equally
attractive. Note the grotesque animal statues on the wall of the park
between the Castle and Cardiff Bridge. Return to the east bank by
suspension footbridge.

Easy wide paths lead along the riverbank, under Gabalfa Bridge
(detour for Llandaff Cathedral possible here) to the new Llandaff
Bridge. Turn away from the river after some rugby pitches and make
for a road going under a railway bridge. The next half mile is industrial but has some interest. First is the very tidy refuse disposal
depot. Just beyond the Atlas Express depot a slight detour reveals an
old water wheel in process of renovation. The ugly building beyond is
the Melingriffydd factory - now an industrial relic. A more attractive
industrial relic which follows is the Glamorgan Canal, now a nature reserve. There is a choice of routes. Ahead to the right a stony drive
is a public footpath leading onto the top of a steep bank of fine old
woodland but the more interesting way is ahead left along the towpath
of the old canal, a botanist's paradise now in the care of the City.
The canal ends abruptly at an approach road to the Coryton interchange
of the M4. This "Spaghetti" junction provides the first real test of
navigation as you negotiate two footbridges and two underpasses -
what fun it must have been planning all this. (See map 1A). However,
that is the last motorway you will see on Cambrian Way. Tongwynlais

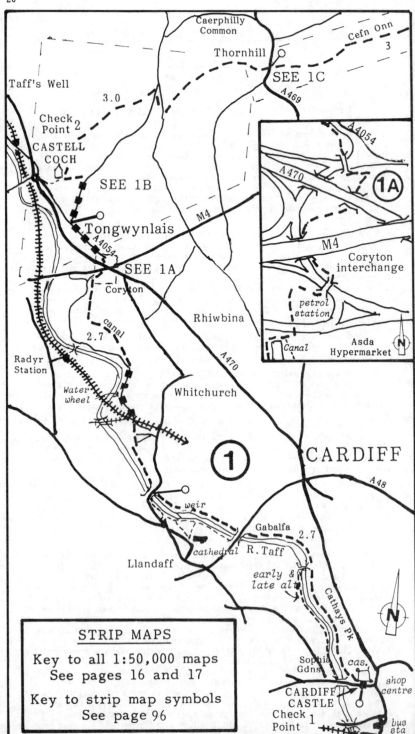

STRIP MAPS

Key to all 1:50,000 maps
See pages 16 and 17

Key to strip map symbols
See page 96

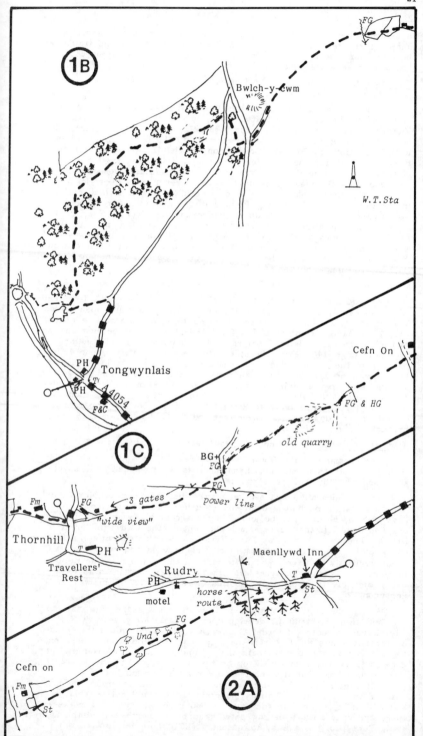

has three pubs, two offering snacks at the bar, and a fish and chip shop. If a late start has been made from Cardiff, buses and trains can be taken for overnight accommodation in Cardiff, or Llwynypia youth hostel (see separate hostel list).

Tongwynlais to Machen   8.3 miles   875 feet of ascent
Maps 1, 1B, 1C, 2, 2A, 2B

Walk up the road to the Castell Coch driveway, ignoring earlier signs off to the left. The castle is a fairy tale style reconstruction of Victorian times, having been a complete ruin in 1870. The internal decor is lavish and worth a visit. A path up the bank behind the car park leads through Forestry Commission woodland. Keep to the main track, which unfortunately offers no views. Follow the inset map, which is shown in more detail near Thornhill where fields are crossed. Near an old quarry the view opens up to reveal Caerphilly with its large castle dimly discernible. The way continues to be well defined except in the wood beyond Cefn On. Beyond Rudry a dead end road leads into woods called Coed Cefn Pwll Du at grid reference 208871. Keep to the main forest road firstly north-east, then north, ignoring the first left forest road shown on the 1:50,000 map. Also ignore the bridleway marked on the map going northwards which does not exist on the ground. A view point with a seat shows the way ahead beyond Machen to Mynydd Machen, the next checkpoint.

Machen to Risca   3 miles   1022 feet of ascent   Maps 2, 2B & 2C

Mynydd Machen, the first definable summit on the route, is ascended by an evenly graded path up through forestry to reach open common. This is the first of several commons encountered on this section where the public have a right of access for "air and exercise" because the land was in an area administered before 1974 by an urban district council (see note page 14). From the stile onto the common there is no defined path up to the summit where there is a trig point and radio station (checkpoint no.3). The fine panorama includes views across the Bristol Channel and up the mining valleys of Rhymney, Ebbw and Sirhowy. The way off is to follow the access road to the radio station, then by field and forest paths down to Risca. The reason for the apparently circuitous way down is that the direct route would be down very steep bracken covered hillside.

Risca to Pontypool   7.8 miles   1504 feet of ascent   Maps 2C, 3 & 3A

The crossing of the Ebbw Valley between Risca and Crosskeys is more populated than was the Rhymney crossing at Machen and as yet accommodation for walkers is sparse.

After a pleasant short section by the disused Monmouthshire and Brecon Canal, a plod up a dead end road leads to common land. At Pegwyn-y-bwlch one may be joined in the ascent of Twmbarlwm by walkers who have left their cars at a high point on the Cwmcarn Forest Drive. The ancient camp at Twmbarlwm is a worthy summit for a further checkpoint. There is a problem of erosion here caused mainly by motor cyclists who have no right to ride on this common. The public, however, has a right of access as this is another common in an ex-urban district. One continues on this common nearly all the way to Pontypool.

Along the length of Mynydd Henllys the view to the right is onto the new town of Cwmbran, developed in the last thirty years. It is the administrative centre of Gwent County. At the point where the forest on the left starts to vere from the ridge my preferred route keeps on the contour on a public footpath that is undefined on the ground, but peak baggers may prefer to keep on the track up to Mynydd Maen See the inset map for the short section off the common before the pleasant edge of common section round the woodlands surrounding the Blaen Blan reservoirs. Thirsty mountain walkers will not be able to resist a visit to a pub with the name of "Mountain Air Inn". The descent to Pontypool is down a narrow gated road to the north-east of the Lamb Inn. Pontypool has a busy town centre (ECD Mon/Thur).

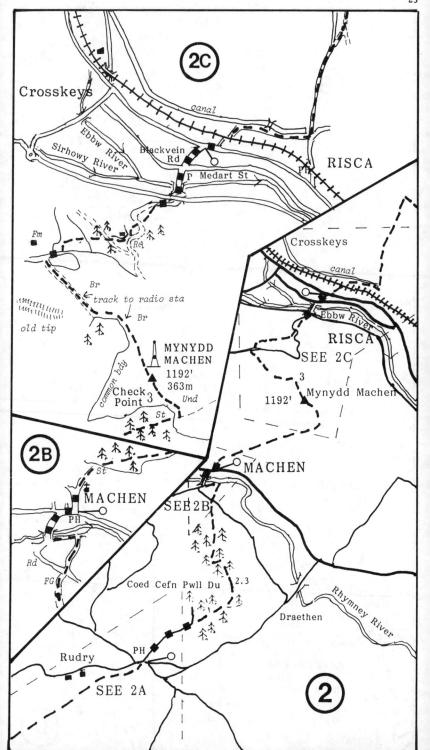

2C

Crosskeys

canal

RISCA

Ebbw River

Sirhowy River

Blackvein Rd

P Medart St

PH

Fm

Rd

Br

track to radio sta

Br

old tip

MYNYDD MACHEN

1192'

363m

Und

common bdy

Check Point 3

St

St

2B

MACHEN

PH

Rd

FG

Coed Cefn Pwll Du

2.3

Rudry

PH

SEE 2A

SEE 2B

MACHEN

Crosskeys

canal

PH

Ebbw River

RISCA

SEE 2C

3

Mynydd Machen

1192'

Draethen

Rhymney River

2

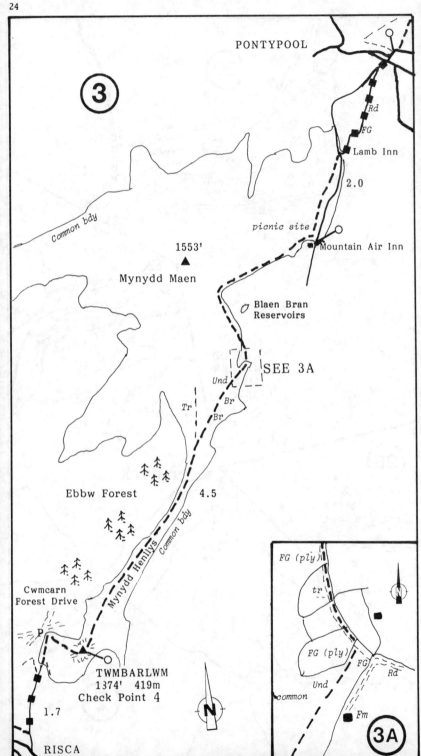

PONTYPOOL

③

Rd

FG

Lamb Inn

2.0

picnic site

Mountain Air Inn

1553'
▲
Mynydd Maen

Blaen Bran
Reservoirs

SEE 3A

Und

Br

Tr

Br

Ebbw Forest

4.5

Cwmcarn
Forest Drive

P

Mynydd Henllys Common bdy

TWMBARLWM
1374' 419m
Check Point 4

1.7

N

RISCA

FG (ply)

tr

N

FG (ply)

FG

Rd

Und

common

Fm

③A

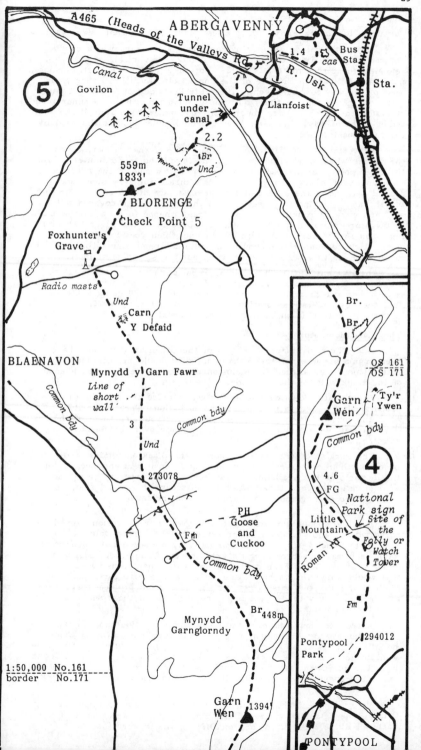

A465 (Heads of the Valleys Rd)
ABERGAVENNY

Canal
Govilon
① 5

Tunnel
under
canal

1.4
cas
Bus
Sta

R. Usk
Llanfoist

Sta.

2.2
Br
Und

559m
1833'

BLORENGE
Check Point 5

Foxhunter's
Grave

Radio masts

Und
Carn
Y Defaid

BLAENAVON

Mynydd y Garn Fawr
Line of
short
wall

Common bdy

3

Common bdy

Und

273078

PH
Goose
and
Cuckoo

Fm

Common bdy

Mynydd
Garnglorndy

Br 448m

Garn
Wen 1394'

Br.
Br.

OS 161
OS 171

Garn
Wen

Ty'r
Ywen

Common bdy

④ 4

4.6
FG

National
Park sign

Little
Mountain

Site of
the
Folly or
Watch
Tower

Roman

Fm

Pontypool
Park

294012

PONTYPOOL

1:50,000 No.161
border No.171

Pontypool to Abergavenny   11.3 miles   1691 ft. of ascent   Maps 4&5.

The most pleasant amenity of Pontypool is the Park which can be entered by the palatial ornamental gates and a detour can be made, rejoining the direct route at 294012. For the direct route mostly enclosed paths are followed to the site of the Pontypool Folly. From there, for most of the way to Abergavenny the route lies along open common land with easy going for the first four miles, but after crossing a minor road at 273078 the going is over rough stony ground with no sign of the public right of way, then over heather and boulder land to the road by the radio masts.

Before taking the path from the east side of the car park, view the plaque which marks the grave of the famous horse Foxhunter. From the trig. point summit head north-east for half a mile to the spectacular viewpoint over Abergavenny. There is a direct but very steep and eroded path down the centre of a north-east face of Blorenge but a better way is just north of east, down through bracken covered hillside and curving round to an isolated tree, whence follow a narrow path to the aforementioned direct way down. Descent to the River Usk crossing is on the line of an old tramway incline which goes in a tunnel where it passes under the Monmouthshire and Brecon Canal (but do diverge to see this beautiful canal from north east end of tunnel).

Abergavenny (ECD Thur.) is an important gateway from England into South Wales, and abounds in B.&B. and eating places. The B.&B. is mostly in two areas of the town, namely (1) on A40 going south-east, near the bus and railway stations and (2) on A40 going west. The information bureau (i on map) is at the bus station.

The Black Mountains

Since the early planning stages of the Cambrian Way there have been arguments whether the Black Mountains should be included. The writer has always argued for inclusion because of the sheer excellence of the ridge walking they provide.

The Countryside Commission at first included them in the draft proposals but bowed to pressure from the National Park authority. When the project officer was appointed for the southern third of the Way, he was not asked to investigate any route over the Black Mountains.

The Park's reasons for exclusion of the Black Mountains were based on their conservation importance and sensitivity and because of the de facto access availability to walkers. This seems to be a "can't win" situation since if there had been no access this would also, no doubt, have been given as a reason for non-inclusion.

The Black Mountains have suffered greatly from erosion caused by horse riding, and only to a lesser extent by the feet of walkers. The descent to Capel-y-ffin has been wrecked by horses and the summit of Waun Fach may never recover its grass cover. The eroded slopes of Sugar Loaf and Waun Fach can be by-passed without causing such wear that would widen the gashes. One must accept a bare earth path for much of the way but this is not the sort of erosion problem that besets the Pennine Way with its peat bogs, nor will use of these sections wear away the mountains.

A frequent criticism of inclusion of the Black Mountains is that two days after leaving Abergavenny one is only four miles away at Crickhowell. This is a valid point and aggravating to the beeliners who only want to get from one end of Wales to the other, to say they have "done it". For our Connoisseur of mountain walking the quality of the walking and the scenery is what counts. It would be a crime to omit the Black Mountains.

Many prospective Cambrian Way walkers will have followed the Offa's Dyke Path and will recall trudging along the twelve miles of the Hatterall Ridge. It's hard luck on Offa's Dyke walkers that their

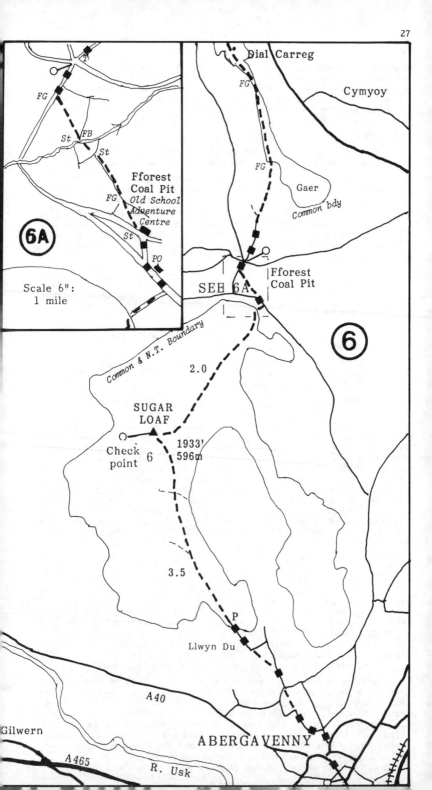

Dial Carreg

Cymyoy

FG

FG

Gaer

Common bdy

Fforest
Coal Pit

(6A)

FG

St *FB*

St

Fforest
Coal Pit
*Old School
Adventure
Centre*

FG

St

PO

Scale 6":
1 mile

SEE 6A

(6)

Common & N.T. Boundary

2.0

SUGAR
LOAF

▲

1933'
596m

Check
point 6

3.5

P

Llwyn Du

A40

Gilwern

A465

R. Usk

ABERGAVENNY

route follows the longest and least interesting of the Black Mountain
ridges. Cambrian Way follows most of the good ridges, but never for
too long in one direction or without some up and down. Whereas the
slopes of the Hatterall Ridge curve to prevent views into the valleys
immediately below, the opposite is true of the Bal Mawr and Pen Allt-
mawr ridges from which both near and distant views are superb.

Alternative Routes to Black Mountains

     If despite the foregoing paragraphs the reader decides to by-pass
the Black Mountains, there are several possibilities, as follows:-

     1. From Blorenge to Mynydd Llangattock, crossing the B4246
     at Pen-ffordd-goch Pond (255108) and proceeding across open
     common land to Llam-march and to Cwm Clydach national nature
     reserve. The dramatic gorge is crossed by the Devil's Bridge
     thence by subway under the Heads of the Valleys road (A465) to
     the Drum and Monkey Inn at Blackrock. The escarpment of the
     east and north sides of Mynydd Llangattock can be followed to
     rejoin the main route at Daren Cilau (200159).

     2. The towpath of the Brecon and Usk Canal can be followed
     from the tunnel referred to in the text at 285130 to Llangattock,
     near Crickhowell. Said to be the most attractive canal in Britain,
     it has been much restored for pleasure boating and its towpath
     is well maintained by the national park authority. On this six
     mile stretch the canal twists and turns as it follows the contours
     round the hillside some 150 to 200 feet above the river Usk, with
     consequent good views across the valley.

     3. From the summit of Sugar Loaf to Crickhowell either via
     Mynydd Pen-y-fal and Llangenny or via Cwm Gwenffrwd, Cwrt-y-
     gollen and riverside walk to Crickhowell Bridge.

Abergavenny to Capel-y-ffin via Sugar Loaf and Bal Mawr   13 miles
                  3443 feet of ascent   Maps 6 to 8

     The recommended way out of Abergavenny from the Town Hall
Clock Tower is along the main street, thence via Pound Road and Avenue
Road to Llwyn Du. One is spoilt for choice as to ways up Sugar Loaf
from Abergavenny. There are pleasant routes up the east side of the
Rholben ridge and up the ridge itself but my preferred route is up St.
Mary's Vale on the west side of that ridge. The path ascends gradually
from a small car park onto the open bracken covered common. Sugar
Loaf has public right of access both because it is a common in a former
urban district and because it is National Trust land open to the public.
Keep on ascending path until the broad ridge is gained then follow paths
to the summit, avoiding the badly eroded south-west flank (which leads
in from the highest car park).

     Leave Sugar Loaf by the north-east ridge again taking care not to
cause further erosion near the top. A short lane connects the common
to a minor road at Fforest Coal Pit (charcoal, not the black variety)
whence paths and minor roads are followed to Dialgarreg where the
splendour of the Black Mountain ridges begins to be apparent as one
looks down on the right to the Vale of Ewyas and to the left the forested Grwyne Fawr. Across the former valley is the crooked church at
Cwmyoy, where the chancel tilts one way and the tower another. In
the latter valley, and worth a detour from the cross roads at Fforest if
time permits, is the isolated church of Partrishow, noted for its rood
loft with beautiful carved oak screen, and nearby holy well.

     Continuing over Garn Wen to Bal Mawr, the ridge becomes narrower
and the views improve into the contrasting valleys on either side. About
half a mile after passing the forest turn right for Capel-y-ffin at a
stone called the Blacksmith's Anvil. The way is at first none too apparent
but where the descent gets steeper the mess that horse riding has made
of the way down is only too obvious. Pass between The Grange (B.&B.
and inquiries about camping further on) and the former monastery, and
so to Capel-y-ffin (the chapel on the border). (Check Point No. 7.)
This idyllic spot at the junction of steep sided valleys was initially

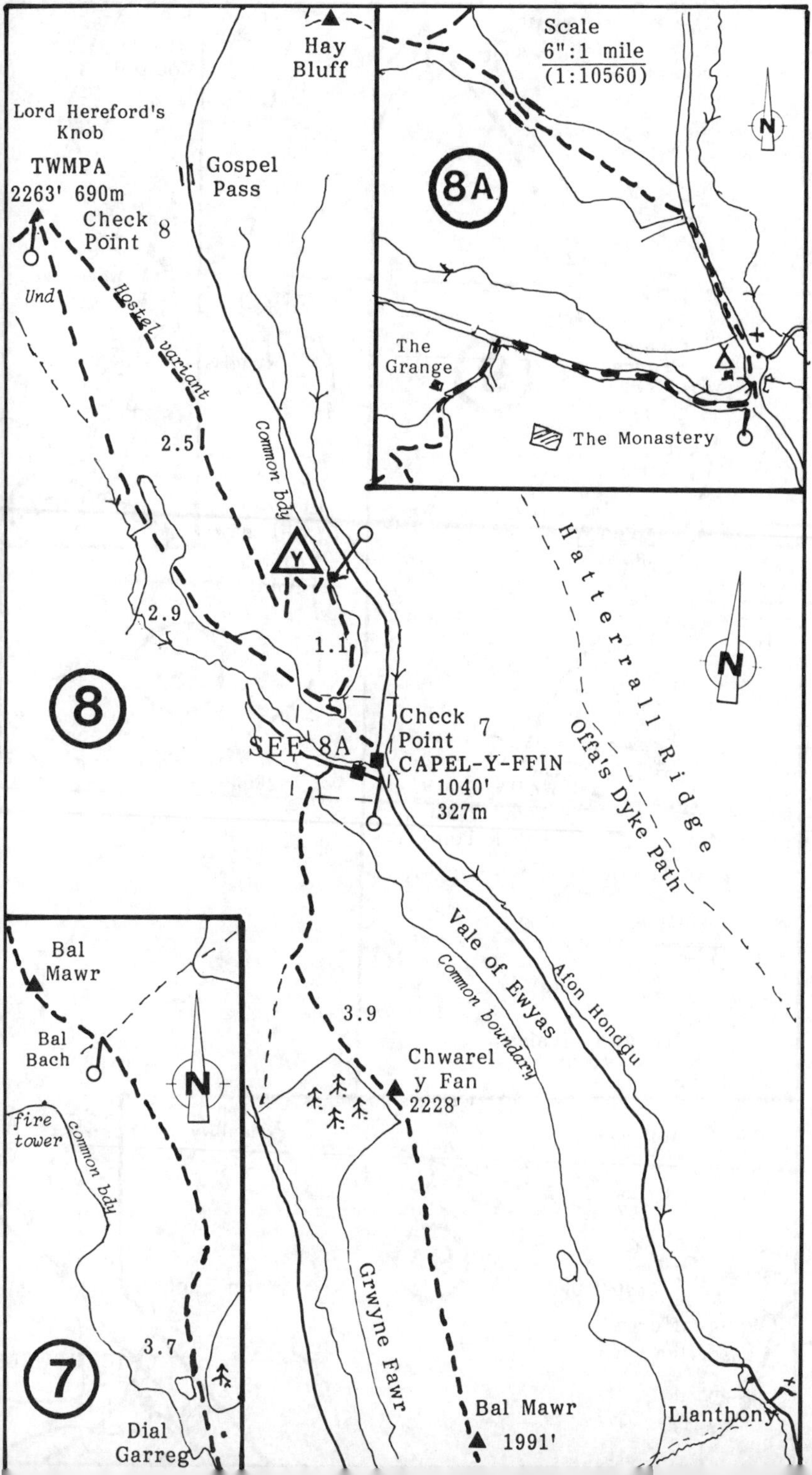

Hay Bluff

Lord Hereford's Knob
TWMPA
2263' 690m
Check Point 8

Und

Gospel Pass

Hostel variant

2.5

2.9

Common bdy

1.1

Scale
6":1 mile
(1:10560)

8A

The Grange

The Monastery

SEE 8A

Check Point
CAPEL-Y-FFIN
1040'
327m

Hatterrall Ridge

Offa's Dyke Path

Vale of Ewyas

Common boundary

Afon Honddu

Bal Mawr

Bal Bach

fire tower

common bdy

3.7

7

Dial Garreg

3.9

Chwarel y Fan
2228'

Grwyne Fawr

Bal Mawr
1991'

Llanthony

8

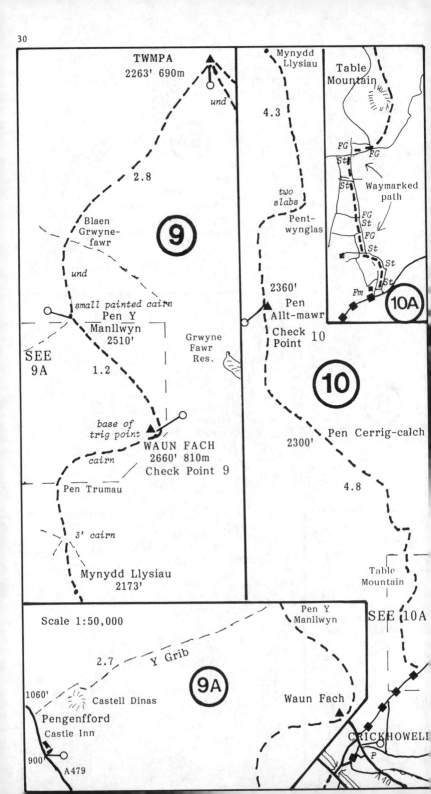

TWMPA
2263' 690m

und

2.8

Blaen
Grwyne-
fawr

und

9

small painted cairn
Pen Y
Manllwyn
2510'

SEE
9A

1.2

*base of
trig point*

WAUN FACH
2660' 810m
Check Point 9

cairn

Pen Trumau

3' cairn

Mynydd Llysiau
2173'

Mynydd
Llysiau

Table
Mountain

4.3

*two
slabs*

Pent-
wynglas

2360'
Pen
Allt-mawr
Check
Point 10

Grwyne
Fawr
Res.

10

FG   FG
St

St

FG
St
FG
St
St

St
Fm

Waymarked
path

10A

Pen Cerrig-calch

2300'

4.8

Table
Mountain

SEE 10A

Scale 1:50,000

2.7   Y Grib

9A

Pen Y
Manllwyn

1060'   Castell Dinas

Pengenffordd
Castle Inn

900'   A479

Waun Fach

CRICKHOWELL

P

an idea for the starting place for the Cambrian Way. It was soon
apparent that this was no equivalent of Edale and needed easier lines
of communication.

For those anxious to see the impressive ruins of Llanthony Abbey
and prepared to forgo the pleasures of the Bal Mawr ridge a descent
can be made from Bal-bach (273267). After visiting the abbey and possi-
bly calling or staying at the Half Moon Inn, follow the very minor roads
and tracks on the N.E. side of the river Honddu via Broadley and
the Vision Farm to Capel-y-ffin. The main road up the valley is
narrow with high hedges and not recommended for walking.

Capel-y-ffin to Crickhowell via Twmpa, Waun Fach and Pen Allt
Mawr Ridge   16 miles   2652 feet of ascent   Maps 8 to 10

A section of very narrow road and a field path leads back to the
open common whence the main route to Twmpa and the hostel variant
divide. If going to the hostel, this way is preferable to the suicidal
road route to the gate below the hostel. The youth hostel is a friendly
old farmhouse with resident warden and is rather special in that it was
provided by the King George VI Memorial Fund, which funded one hostel
each in England, Scotland and Wales. The route from the hostel to
Twmpa is via a steep climb at the back of the hostel and a superb
viewpoint looking down the Vale of Ewyas.

Twmpa, also known as Lord Hereford's Knob, is check point
number 8. This splendid viewpoint on the N.W. escarpment of the
Black Mountains looks out across the wide valley of the Wye to the hills
of central Wales. Two miles away to the N.E. is Hay Bluff - as near as
Cambrian Way goes to the Offa's Dyke Path. In between is the Gospel
Pass over which the icecap of the Great Ice Age overflowed to make the
Vale of Ewyas, the only glaciated valley of the Black Mountains.

From Twmpa to Waun Fach a path is well worn along the open
common except after crossing the old track coming up from Grwyne Fawr
where there are several rival paths. A compass will certainly by needed
in mist.

From just short of Pen y Minllwyn (small painted cairn) a diversion
can be made down Y Grib to Pengenffordd for possible sustenance and/
or camping at the Castle Inn.

The summit of Waun Fawr is on a flat plateau and not exactly impressive as the highest point in the Black Mountains. It is check point
number 9 but our mountain Connoisseur is excused having to walk to
the actual base of the former trig. point provided a wide circuit is
taken round it, well beyond the summit area, which is devoid of veget-
ation due to too many feet both human and equine.

The eroded parts of the slope going westwards from Waun Fach
can be by-passed without causing more erosion. Superb ridge walking
follows over Mynydd Llysiau, Pen Allt-mawr and Pen Cerrig-calch before
descent to the curious Table Mountain, an iron age hill fort, which is
aptly named. The open common is left just below Table Mountain at
225203 and waymarked field paths followed (see map 10A) to a road
leading into Crickhowell.

Crickhowell is a small town with many scheduled buildings. One of
these was the youth hostel but regrettably serious structural defects
were discovered which were beyond the resources of the Y.H.A. to
remedy, causing its closure in 1982. There is, however, ample B.&B.,
a good camp site, and many pubs.

Crickhowell to Storey Arms via Mynydd Llangynidr and Pen y Fan
20 miles   4896 feet of ascent   Maps 11 to 15

Crickhowell Bridge, over the Usk, is a gem of an old stone bridge.
From it a path leads over fields to Llangattock church and thence up
to the Brecon and Usk Canal, the towpath of which is followed for half
a mile, as far as the second bridge. An old tramway route, at first
on the flat, then up a steep incline leads to Llangattock Quarries. The
next two miles provide some of the most spectacular scenery on the whole

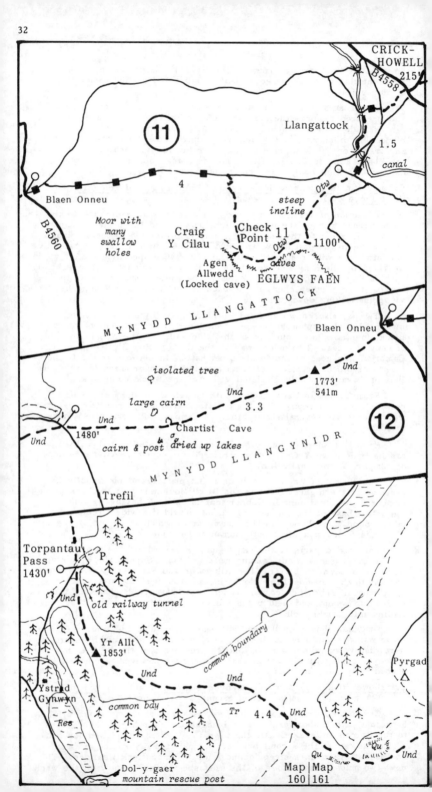

Cambrian Way. The area is a nature reserve. An old tramway route on a ledge below Darren Cilau leads to a spot where a short scramble gives access into a large open cave, Eglwys Faen, which can be explored with a torch. (Check point no. 11.) A different proposition is Agen Allwedd cave which is many miles long and only accessible to those with a key. Near to Agen Allwedd entrance a path gradually descends off the main ledge to the base of the cliff and to an area of springs and swamp before reaching the Llangattock - Blaen Onneu road.

From the road junction at Blaen Onneu across Mynydd Llangynidr is a very wild and open moor, over which careful navigation is essential, even in good visibility. This is cave country with many swallow holes and sheep tracks, but few defined paths. The rights of way do not help but de facto access is traditional here.

The first objective is the trig. point at 148159 but more difficult to find is the Chartist Cave, where clandestine presses printed forbidden political papers nearly a century and a half ago. Cairns and an isolated tree provide clues but in mist only good compass and contour navigation will enable the socialist pilgrim to find the wide open cave, facing south, and appreciate this inhospitable shelter. If the cave can be easily missed at least one should strike the road to Trefil quarries. After a slight detour to look down into the very steep sided valley of Dyffryn Crawnon, take a line to the upper side of the large quarry and continue, still on open common on undefined route and make for the ridge of Yr Allt and so down to Torpantau Pass.

From Torpantau to Pen y Fan, the highest point in the Brecon Beacons, the obvious and popular route is via Craig y Fan-ddu, Craig Cwareli and Cribin. The first of several eroded sections on this route is the ascent of Craig y Fan-ddu. This seems to have been aggravated by putting a car park in the forest near Torpantau Pass, but our Cambrian Way walker will add little to the erosion if discretion is exercised in using either the worn track or avoiding it. At a stream (050192) a line is struck across the wild moorland top for half a mile to meet the crag-top path of Craig Cwareli. From here to Pen y Fan and on to Storey Arms, the paths are all very well worn, including short cuts of Fan Big and Cribin. The purists will visit all the summits but only Pen y Fan has been made a check point so as not to discourage the less eroded alternative described below. It is the south-east ridge of Pen y Fan which provides the National Park with its most intractable erosion problem, and which seems only likely to be solved by a concession to artificiality in some form of steps if the mountain is not to be gradually worn away. However Pen y Fan will not disappear for a few million years yet, so if you want to follow the most spectacular crag-top route in the Brecon Beacons you must accept the erosion eyesores and your contribution to gradual lowering of the mountains.

The alternative between Torpantau and Pen y Fan is along the long and less interesting cragtop ridge accessible from the base of the lower Neuadd reservoir and passing along Craig Fan Ddu (no connection with crag in last paragraph), Craig Gwaun-taf and Duwynt (824m). This route, often used as a return on a horseshoe ascent of Pen y Fan from Torpantau, was put forward in Mr. Tetlow's report as a suggested route for Cambrian Way. The owners, National Trust and Forestry Commission, were said to be agreeable. There was a naive assumption that the summit of Pen y Fan would be by-passed, but at least if it is visited the south-east ridge is avoided.

There is no need to follow the grossly overused and eroded path from Bwlch Duwynt to the A470 at Pont ar Daf. More rewarding is to come off the west side of the plateau summit of Corn Du and follow the north-west ridge down to an obelisk. This is a memorial to Tommy Jones who, aged five, got lost while staying at a farm in the valley, and whose body was found at that spot nearly a month later. Cross the valley to a ladder stile or take a wide sweep round the head of the valley, and so by path down to Storey Arms. The former pub which gave its name to this important road pass is long since gone so that you are more likely to get sustenance from an ice cream van.

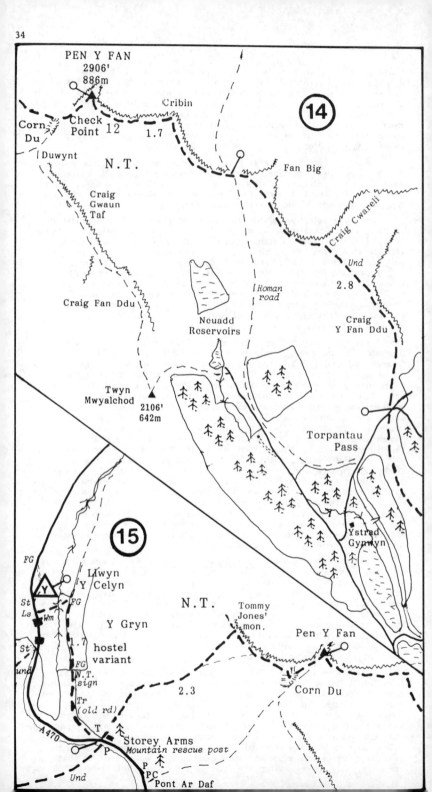

Part of the Youth Adventure Centre at Storey Arms used to be a youth hostel but now the hostel in this area is two miles towards Brecon in less bleak surroundings. It has been converted to a hostel from a farmhouse and barns. A quieter route to it than the busy trunk road is along the old road on the east side of the valley and then by a permissive route across National Trust land from 977222 to 972221.

Storey Arms to Llandovery via Fforest Fawr and the Carmarthen Vans

| 22.6 miles | 4955 feet of ascent | Maps 16 to 20 |

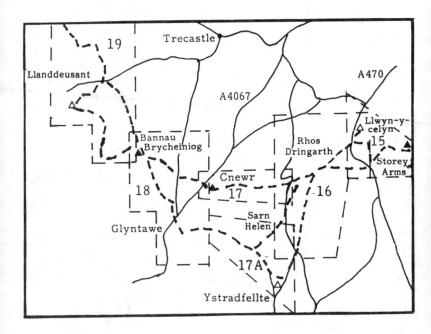

Map showing the relationship of the alternative routes between the Brecon Beacons and the Carmarthen Vans, and the strip maps involved.

Fforest Fawr (Great Forest) is not forest in the modern sense but a large open moor. The first section traversed lies between the Brecon to Merthyr road (A470) and the minor road from Heol Senni to Ystradfellte. Another large section is on the east side of the main ridge of the Carmarthen Vans with Bannau Brycheiniog part way along its open boundary with the Black Mountain common. These enormous commons are used for grazing by many farmers from the surrounding area. In February 1984, the National Park authority purchased the eastern part and several other sections from the Eagle Star Insurance Company for £30,000, with the help of grants from the National Heritage Memorial Fund and the Countryside Commission. The purpose of this very welcome purchase was to protect the commons, to conserve the open hill landscape and also the access on foot which the public has enjoyed in practice, if not as of right, for many years.

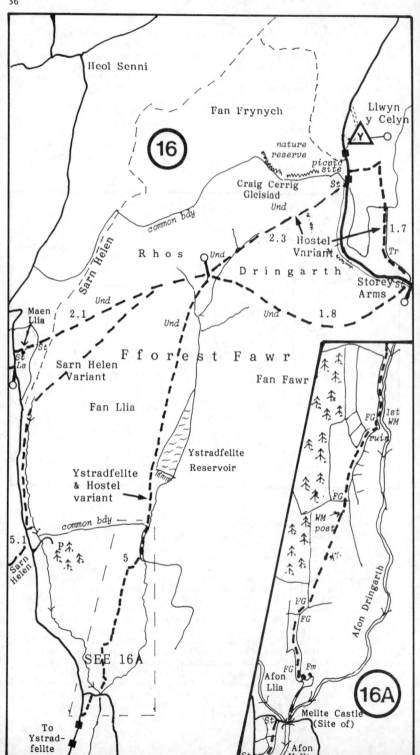

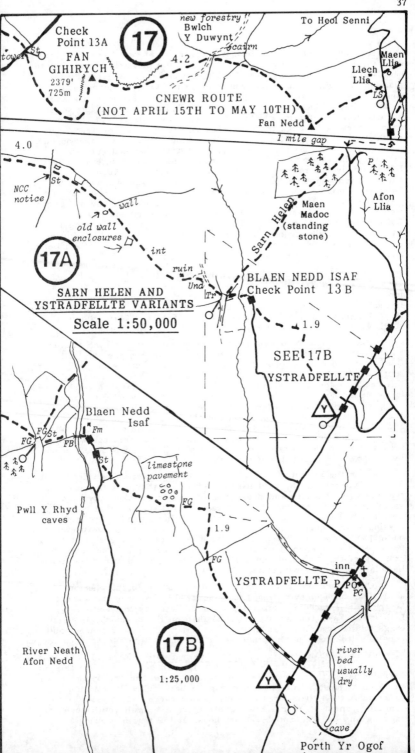

Check Point 13A
FAN GIHIRYCH
2379' 725m

⑰

new forestry
Bwlch Y Duwynt
cairn

To Heol Senni

Maen Llia

Llech Llia

LS

4.2

CNEWR ROUTE
(NOT APRIL 15TH TO MAY 10TH)

Fan Nedd

tower St

1 mile gap

4.0

St

NCC notice

old wall enclosures

wall

int

ruin

Und

Tr

Sarn Helen

Maen Madoc
(standing stone)

P

Afon Llia

⑰A

**SARN HELEN AND
YSTRADFELLTE VARIANTS**

Scale 1:50,000

BLAEN NEDD ISAF
Check Point 13 B

1.9

**SEE 17B
YSTRADFELLTE**

⚠Y

FG St
FG FB
Fm

**Blaen Nedd
Isaf**

St

limestone pavement

FG

Pwll Y Rhyd
caves

FG

1.9

FG

YSTRADFELLTE P PO
PC

inn

⑰B

**River Neath
Afon Nedd**

1:25,000

1.9

⚠Y

river bed usually dry

cave

Porth Yr Ogof

The Cnewr Estate. In the north centre of Fforest Fawr, and including the natural east/west walking route, is the privately owned enclosed
moorland of the Cnewr Estate. Lambing on sheep farms generally takes
place in late winter, near to farmhouses in the valleys, but when the
Cnewr land was first enclosed many years ago the estate had no land
in the valleys. Lambing was therefore carried out in springtime on the
open mountain. Due to possible disturbance by walkers and risk of
sheep worrying by dogs the estate has generally not encouraged access
particularly at lambing time. When the estate applied for permission to
plant parts of the moor with conifers in 1980 the national park made a
deal with the estate to reduce its demands and to allow access across
the estate by two routes, including an east/west route via Fan Nedd,
Fan Gihirych and Cefn Cul. Details of the route were announced in
February 1984. Access is however not allowed between April 15th and
May 10th during the lambing season and is not allowed at night. Organised parties have to notify the National Park Authority in advance.
Dogs must be kept on leads and no fires are permitted. Camping for
backpackers is allowed near the ruined building of Llech Llia. During
the lambing season a detour can be made via the Roman road Sarn Helen
and Glyntawe, or the journey broken at Ystradfellte.

Storey Arms or Llwyn-y-celyn to Rhos Dringarth. Map 16.
Both Cnewr and Ystradfellte routes leave Storey Arms and head west
for Fan Fawr which can be ascended or by-passed on the northern side.
If coming from Llwyn-y-celyn youth hostel, leave the hostel grounds at
the S.W. corner and follow roadside verge of A470. Climb obliquely
south-west onto the wide expanse of Rhos Dringarth.

Rhos Dringarth to Bannau Brycheiniog via Fan Gihirych (Cnewr
Estate) maps 16, 17 and 18. (Not between April 15th and May 10th.)
Once on the broad expanse of the rhos (moorland) strike generally
south westwards. From the broad ridge between Cefn Perfedd and Fan
Llia head for the large standing stone, Maen Llia. A rough track, which
is an old Roman road called Sarn Helen, is crossed shortly before reaching a wall. This is the edge of the Cnewr Estate. A new stile invites
one to cross the small enclosed section of moor to the standing stone
and thence over a stile onto the Heol Senni to Ystradfellte road. A few
yards south a ladder stile indicates the start of the permissive route
across the Cnewr moors. Head for the summit of Fan Nedd, then north
west to Bwlch y Duwynt and Fan Gihirych.

From the summit of Fan Gihirych there is a very steep descent to
Bwlch Bryn-rhudd, the road pass on A4067, so that it is necessary in
the interests of safety and prevention of erosion to follow the edge
southwards until the slope becomes easier and then to strike north-
west to the bwlch. The route continues on Cnewr land over Cefn Cul
passing near a curious tower. Old walls and fence posts are useful for
navigation across the bleak moor, and it is important to arrive at the
ladder stile near Maen Mawr stone circle because there is no other
crossing of the high wall and barbed wire fence which marks the western
boundary of the Cnewr Estate. (853203).

Once again one is on open land of the Great Forest where de facto
access has been enjoyed from time immemorial. Crossing the Tawe can
be tricky - if necessary cross higher up. Head for the south end of
Llyn y Fan Fawr (not visible at first) then on the obvious path up the
crags to the summit of Bannau Brycheiniog, 2630 feet/802 metres, and
hopefully look back to the other peaks that have been ascended en route.

Alternative routes avoiding the Cnewr Estate. Maps 16, 17A & 18.
1. Via Ystradfellte. If an extra day can be spared then this
variation is worth while on its own account because of the opportunity
to spend at least a half day exploring the beautiful valleys around
Ystradfellte with their famous waterfalls and caves. This assumes that
a night is spent at Ystradfellte, where there is a small youth hostel and
camping and one bed and breakfast house at the time of writing.

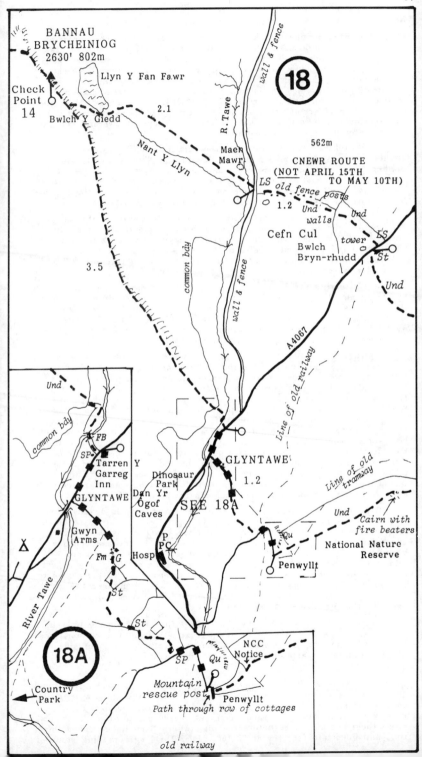

From Rhos Dringarth take a wide sweep round the moor, crossing several small tributaries of the Dringarth and then head south to pass along the west side of the Ystradfellte reservoir. Once past the dam drop down to the river and where a fence comes down from the west, turn alongside the river at 943168 and scramble between the river and the fence for about 400 yards to a gate where a waymarked public footpath starts, near Blaen-tringarth at 942164. This is the only right of way off this part of the common and must be followed precisely. The waymarking is yellow Countryside Commission shape arrows and ends at the road by the site of Mellte Castle.

Ystradfellte. The solubility of the carboniferous limestone hereabouts has caused the rivers Mellte, Hepste and Nedd (Neath) to go underground, sometimes completely and in other parts for all except flood time. Alternate layers of hard and soft rocks have also caused waterfalls. Add to that the steep sided valleys clothed in natural woodlands and you have a wonderland of great interest and beauty.

If arriving from the Storey Arms area in the middle of the day one can, before spending the night, have a rewarding half day proceeding down the Mellte valley via Porth yr Ogof (large open cave) and the three Clun Gwyn falls to Sgwd yr Eira on the Hepste river. This latter is a waterfall with a public footpath that passes between the waterfall and the cliff it shoots over.

If two nights can be spent at Ystradfellte, a day is recommended exploring also the valleys of the Nedd, Sychryd and Pyrddin, especially if the rivers are low enough for walking along riverbeds. See Chris Barber's book "Exploring the Brecon Beacons National Park". The cave systems should be treated with great respect, and only entered by experienced cavers with the appropriate equipment.

Ystradfellte to Glyntawe. Routes from the youth hostel and from the area of the pub, post office and church converge in a field at 920139 and then go west, past an interesting limestone pavement on the way to Blaen Nedd Isaf Farm. Go through a gate at the south end of the row of buildings. Sarn Helen, an old Roman road is crossed at 908144. Here starts a public footpath that traverses a wild open moor without touching any other highway for four miles. The 1:50,000 map shows little to guide one but the walls and small enclosures on the sketch map should more than suffice for navigation. The western half of the path is through a national nature reserve noted for its cave systems. The path terminates in a tunnel through the middle of a line of cottages all of which form a caving centre for the South Wales Caving Club. A disused railway is crossed and a signpost followed on what appears to be an unofficial diversion at the start of a path down to Glyntawe.

Glyntawe, apart from being a scattered community in a very attractive valley, is noteworthy for the Dan yr Ogof Caves, claimed to be the largest showcave complex in Europe, and for Craig y nos Castle, an enormous Gothic style chateau where, at the turn of the last century Madame Adelina Patti, the famous opera singer provided lavish entertainment and was a frequent host to royalty. The castle is now a geriatric hospital but most of the fine grounds form a country park open to the public. An alternative path from Penwyllt via Rhongyr-uchaf gives access to the park at 843157. If time permits the caves should be visited and also the life size dinosaur park.

Glyntawe to Bannau Brycheiniog. Opposite the Tafarn-y-Garreg Inn a path leads to a fine new footbridge and then on a diversion leading to the open common at 848173. The rough stone strewn hillside is climbed and the escarpment followed for three miles to its highest point at Bannau Brycheiniog.

2. Alternative to the Cnewr Estate via Sarn Helen. If seeking to avoid the Cnewr Estate but not wishing to go to Ystradfellte, take a more south-westerly line from Rhos Dringarth so as to hit the Heol Senni road where it is joined by Sarn Helen, at 925184 or, if Afon Llia is low, cross the river anywhere before reaching where Sarn Helen leaves the road and goes into forestry at 926166. Pass the large standing stone of

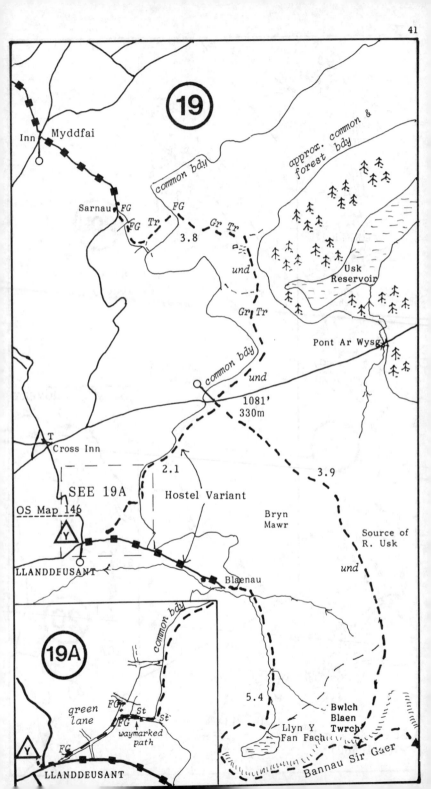

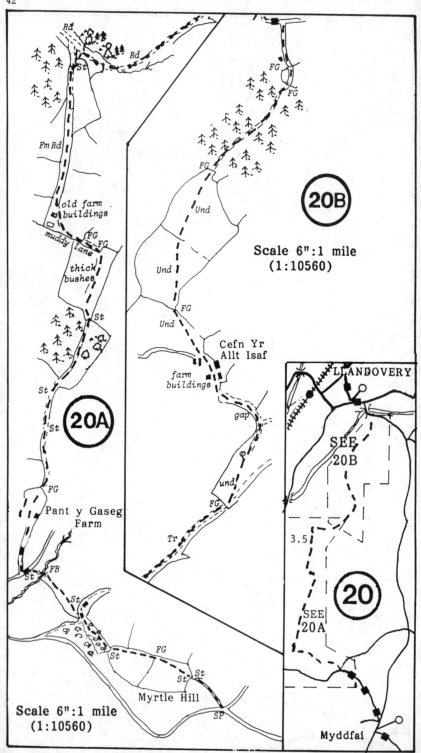

20A

20B

Scale 6":1 mile
(1:10560)

Scale 6":1 mile
(1:10560)

Rd

Rd

St

FG

FG

FG

Fm Rd

old farm
buildings

Und

FG
FG

muddy lane

thick
bushes

Und

St

FG

Und

St

Cefn Yr
Allt Isaf

St

farm
buildings

St

gap

FG

und

Pant y Gaseg
Farm

FG

St FB

Tr

St

St

FG

St

St

Myrtle Hill

SP

LLANDOVERY

SEE
20B

20

3.5

SEE
20A

Myddfai

Maen Madoc and join the Ystradfellte to Glyntawe route near Blaen Nedd Isaf Farm at 908144.

The Carmarthen Vans (Van = peak). I have always understood the term Carmarthen Vans to refer to the mountain range marked on the maps as the Black Mountain and the western end of Fforest Fawr. The Black Mountain (not to be confused with the Black Mountains at the other end of the national park) was in the county of Carmarthen (Sir Gaer), now part of Dyfed county. The Fforest Fawr section was in the county of Brecknock, also known as Breconshire, and now part of Powys county. Both constitute one enormous open moor to which there has been de facto public access from time immemorial. Farms from some distance around have grazing rights on these two commons. The Black Mountain was acquired by the national park authority in 1988 after abortive purchase by an Egyptian who was unable to complete the purchase and then by an unknown buyer.

The highest part of the mountain range has two principle summits though neither can really be called peaks in the true sense. Bannau Brycheiniog (Brecknock Peaks) is the highest at 2630 feet/802 metres, while the next highest is Bannau Sir Gaer at 2460 feet/750 metres.

The walker may wonder how shepherds find their flocks if the sheep can wander anywhere on such a vast fenceless common. Under the hefting system the sheep get to know their patch and stick to it. They pass on their knowledge to their lambs. Sheep are very lost if driven off their patch and this is one reason why walkers should not have a dog with them. Sheep instinctively run away from a dog, even if it is on a lead. Unless surprised by walkers sheep are generally fairly oblivious to walkers as such and there need be no conflict of interest.

Carmarthen Vans to Llandovery. From the summits of the Carmarthen Vans the recommended route depends on whether the walker needs a roof for the night. The simple youth hostel in the tiny hamlet of Llanddeusant provides the excuse to walk the top of the superb escarpment of Bannau Sir Gaer, overlooking Llyn y Fan Fach and then to drop down to the lake and follow the water board road down to Blaenau (caravans to let) and along a narrow minor road into Llanddeusant. Return route to the common is by grassy lanes.

The main route from Bannau Brycheiniog strikes northwards and continues over open land for another six miles before descending to lower levels with enclosed fields and roads. Avoid the obvious steep and erosion prone nose of Fan Foel and strike westwards to the pass of Bwlch Blaen Twrch at 816218, and down a zig-zag path before heading northwards. Our Mountain Connoisseur is however advised to do the whole circuit of Bannau Sir Gaer and down to Llyn y Fan Fach before contouring round to the direct route. Llyn y Fan Fach is the site of one of the most fascinating of Welsh legends, that of the lady of the lake. See Richard Sale's "A Cambrian Way" and many other books.

The way via the source of the Usk and Bryn Mawr is fairly featureless and expert map and compass work may be necessary. About a mile after crossing the Llanddeusant to Trecastle road the black pecks on the 1:50,000 map do a sharp left turn (802278). Here strike north on an undefined route to join a grass track near a low cairn. The common is left by a grass track down to Sarnau and a narrow road followed to the village of Myddfai. Minor road walking is necessary to Myrtle Hill, whence follow little used tracks and paths to Llandovery. The maps 20A and 20B are six inch to the mile and should ensure lack of navigational problems on this very pleasant section which is in such sharp contrast to the stark open landscapes of the Brecon Beacons.

Llandovery is a natural staging and revictualling point. It has ample accommodation, eating houses, a camp site and a tourist information office. Hostellers will tend to make it a midday call between Llanddeusant and Bryn Poeth. If the Cambrian Way walk is being done in three sections then the railway and coach services to Llandovery will prove useful.

CENTRAL SECTION

LLANDOVERY TO DINAS MAWDDWY
Via the Elenydd and Plynlimon

Distance 77½ miles   Ascent 12666 feet

After a generally east to west traverse of the Brecon Beacons and Black Mountains National Park, our Connoisseur must now set face to the north in earnest. Let it not be thought, however, that the next few days of walking are just a beeline for Snowdonia. For those with a limited knowledge of Wales the central section is likely to be a revelation as to the wildness and beauty that is seen by few visitors to Wales.

The route crosses the Elenydd and Plynlimon ranges, both large and remote areas of mountain and moorland, which though having many crags and outcrops have few spectacular summits. In 1972 the Countryside Commission tried to designate these areas as a national park but there was much opposition locally. Much to the disgust of the Commission, and amenity and tourist interests, the Secretary of State for Wales, without even holding a public inquiry, refused to confirm the designation order. If this area had become a national park 80% of the Cambrian Way would have been in a national park. With hindsight the Commission might have been wiser to have gone for the lower status of an "Area of Outstanding Natural Beauty".

Forestry is the greatest threat to wildlife and amenity interests in this area. The many grants and tax concessions given to commercial tree growing has led to vast areas in the Elenydd being planted with conifers, though rather more on the eastern side than the western. This led Cambrian Way surveyors to suggest a line near the west side of the range, even though this meant omitting the scenic qualities of the Elan Valley reservoirs. In fact only five miles of the route in the central section goes through conifer woodlands.

There are not so many ridges and escarpments to follow in the central section but this is made up for by the attractiveness of the valleys walked, notably the Towy, Doethie and Rheiddol.

Llandovery to Rhandirmwyn   6.6 miles   1033 feet of ascent   Map 21

From Llandovery the next objective is likely to be Rhandirmwyn or Bryn Poeth Youth Hostel. The most obvious ridge north of Llandovery has no public access at all so the choice lies between following the Towy valley by footpaths and roads through Cilycwm village or the recommended more direct route following a very minor road on the east side of Fforest ridge, then an old road and a gated path to point 784418, whence hostellers follow another minor road, with good views to the warden's farmhouse, while others drop down to the Towy itself and follow the river path to Rhandirmwyn.

Rhandirmwyn belies its name, which means "district of mines", for the old lead mines are barely visible in the delectable valley in which this scattered village is situated. The village post office/stores however is a "mine" of information and the Royal Oak a useful inn.

This area is very much R.S.P.B. country, with many species of birds in the woods of the nature reserves. This is a likely area on the Cambrian Way, but not the only place, that you may see a kite, a species that nearly became extinct, but which is now much protected and increasing slowly in numbers. The kite is liable to desert its young if disturbed and a year's brood may be lost. Kites do sometimes nest in the Doethie valley which lies ahead and this led to opposition to Cambrian Way going that way, but all the alternatives suggested could have similar objections, and one at least goes through a nature reserve. The Doethie has a public path along it and is a regular route between the youth hostels of Bryn Poeth and Tyncornel, so seems a reasonable route which at least avoids all nature reserves.

Interesting side excursions can be made to Dinas nature reserve and Llyn Brianne but they involve tourist road walking, and return same way

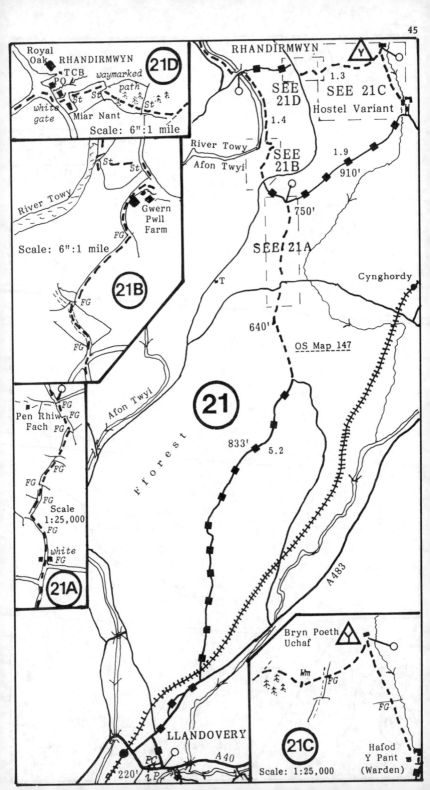

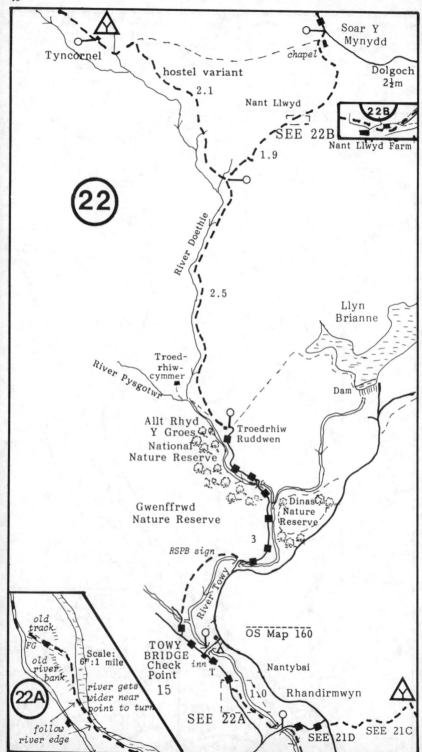

Tyncornel

hostel variant

2.1

Soar Y Mynydd

chapel

Dolgoch 2½m

Nant Llwyd

SEE 22B

1.9

22B

Nant Llwyd Farm

(22)

River Doethie

2.5

Llyn Brianne

Troed-rhiw-cymmer

River Pysgotwr

Dam

Allt Rhyd Y Groes National Nature Reserve

Troedrhiw Ruddwen

Gwenffrwd Nature Reserve

Dinas Nature Reserve

3

RSPB sign

River Towy

OS Map 160

TOWY BRIDGE Check Point 15

inn

Nantybai

Rhandirmwyn

SEE 22A

1.0

SEE 21D

SEE 21C

old track

FG

old river bank

Scale: 6":1 mile

river gets wider near point to turn

(22A)

follow river edge

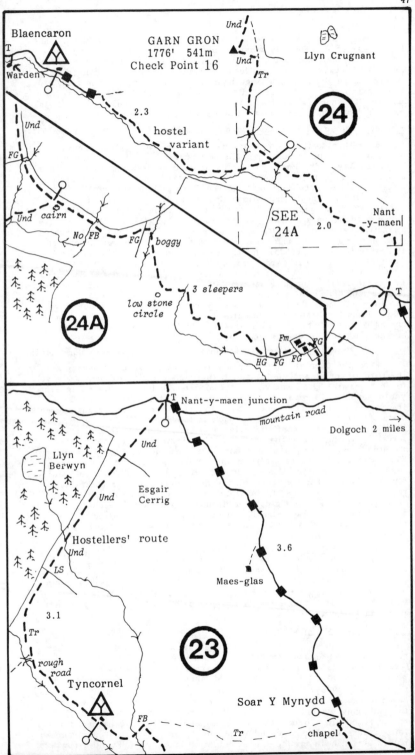

Blaencaron

GARN GRON
1776' 541m
Check Point 16

Llyn Crugnant

T
Warden

Und

2.3

hostel
variant

24

Und

Und

Tr

FG

Und cairn

No FB *FG* boggy

SEE 24A

2.0

Nant
-y-maen

24A

3 sleepers

*low stone
circle*

T

Fm *FG*

HG FG FG

T Nant-y-maen junction

mountain road

Dolgoch 2 miles

Und

Llyn
Berwyn

Esgair
Cerrig

3.6

Maes-glas

Hostellers' route

Und

Und

LS

3.1

23

Tr

*rough
road*

Tyncornel

Soar Y Mynydd

FB

Tr

chapel

if the whole of the Doethie valley is to be walked, as it should be. The Dinas reserve is a densely wooded hill with the rushing Towy on two sides, a circular path round it and a spur up to a cleft known as Twm Shon Catti's cave, where the Welsh equivalent of Robin Hood lived in hiding. Llyn Brianne is a large holding reservoir built in the early '70s. It is an impressive site but it did drown a very attractive wooded valley. The dam, which the author considers the ugliest imaginable, is excused by Richard Sale as a "thoroughly modern dam".

Rhandirmwyn to Nant-y-maen   12 miles   1579 feet of ascent   Maps 22&23.

To return to the main route, we now enter the Doethie valley, which in the author's opinion is the most attractive valley on the whole Cambrian Way. The lower part has extensive natural woods on one side and craggy hillside with scattered trees on the other. A particularly delectable spot is the confluence of the Towy and Doethie with attractive waterfalls. The tarred road ends at Troedrhiw Ruddwen farm. Shortly after, a rough road leads off to Troedrhiwcymmer, but the valley path becomes a grass route, sometimes muddy, but always with attractive valley sides and scattered trees. At 771514 non-hostellers must bear right and climb steeply before descent to the remote chapel at Soar y Mynydd (784533) and thence by minor road to the Tregaron-Abergwesyn road near Nant-y-maen (762577). Hostellers will continue up the valley to Tyncornel, the most remote hostel in Wales. Compared with Bryn Poeth it is more accessible inasmuch as you can get a car to it by a long lonely road from Llandewi Brefi, whereas you can't get a car anywhere near Bryn Poeth, but Tyncornel is much more out in the wild. From the hostel road onwards to Nant y Maen, the route is not on the definitive map of rights of way, but there is a long standing arrangement for its use by hostellers.

Nant-y-maen to Strata Florida   6½ miles   946 feet of ascent   Maps 24&25

From the farm at Nant-y-maen careful navigation is necessary as the path is not always visible and both rough ground and streams have to be crossed. The large cairn at 745595 is the junction for Blaencaron youth hostel and Tregaron. Garn Gron summit, not far off the faint track, though only 1776 feet is a worthy check point, and gives a good distant view on a clear day both back to the Brecon Beacons and on to Plynlimon. The way continues over wild open country, though with forestry growing up to the east. At 738623 the diversion for Pont-rhydfendigaid divides from the main route heading for Strata Florida. The latter route crosses a stream and enters new forestry. By arrangement with the Forestry Commission the author has waymarked the route as far as Talwrn. The way through the dangerous buildings at Talwrn, marked by black dashes on the O.S. map, is said to be a right of way and agreement has been given for its use. Just before reaching the abbey remains at Strata Florida a deep stream has taken over the enclosed footpath and in most seasons the water is well over boot level, so be prepared.

A visit to Pontrhydfendigaid (Bridge at the ford of the Blessed One) may be desirable for replenishing stores and for the bird watcher could be a place for a rest day, with a visit to Tregaron Bog, a national nature reserve nearby. The Heddle tea rooms/B.&B. has been found to be very hospitable and there is a camp site, shop and pubs. A footpath on the north side of the Teifi returns the walker to the main route at Strata Florida.

Strata Florida to Cwmystwyth   9 miles   1408 feet of ascent   Maps 26 & 27.

The remains of Strata Florida Abbey are open to the public. The route follows an ancient monks' route across wild moorlands to Abbey Cwmhir which is a road as far as Ty'n-y-cwm. A turn off is made below Llyn Egnant, one of the series of wild lakes known as Teifi Pools. From there nearly to Cwmystwyth one is on land with a public right of access either because it is on Crown common or because it is on land within the gathering grounds of the Elan Valley reservoirs which are subject to the famous Birmingham Clauses (see page   ). There is no defined route across the wild moorland to get to Domen Milwyn, our next checkpoint, but Claerdu farmbuildings and three lakes, Llyn Fyrddin Fawr,

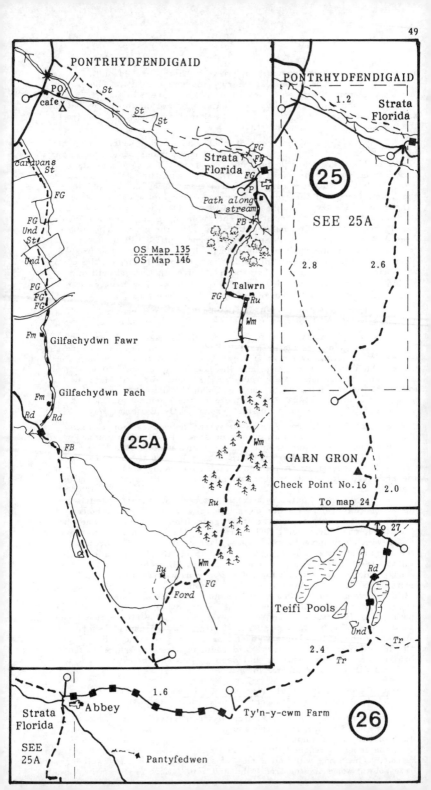

and Fach and Llyn Du provide landmarks. The watershed of the
gathering grounds is marked at intervals by stone pillars. The panorama from Domen Milwyn on a clear day is even more wild than Garn
Gron. A public footpath which terminates nowhere on the right hand
side of Nant Milwyn becomes a track further down and takes one from
the common down to Cwmystwyth.

Cwmystwyth was the scene of much lead mining, which was in its
heyday at the end of the last century. The enormous mine buildings,
closed in 1921, are one mile up the valley from the village and stand as
a monstrous eyesore or gaunt industrial relic according to taste.
Those with time to spare can keep north from Domen Milwyn and ford
the Ystwyth to visit the ruins but beware - the buildings are very
dangerous. See Simon Hughes "The Cwmystwyth Mine" (published by
Northern Mine Research Society). The river below the mine has incidentally been irrevocably polluted by water from the mine. The village
itself has attractive surroundings and the post office will be a sure call
for supplies and information. Mr. Donald Hoare, who was the project
officer appointed by the Countryside Commission to report on the central
section of the Cambrian Way (see page 7) lives in Cwmystwyth and is
willing to advise walkers and hear of any problems they have encountered. He can be contacted at the Old School (see map).

Cwmystwyth to Dyffryn Castell via Devil's Bridge and Ponterwyd
10½ miles   1930 feet of ascent   Maps 28 & 29

From the Cwmystwyth area it is possible to make a beeline for
Plynlimon by going via Llethr Nant-Hylles or Myherin Forest and crossing
the A44 at Eisteddfa Gurig or Dyffrym Castell, but this route would omit
the spectacular Rheiddol gorge and the fascinating areas of Devil's
Bridge and Ystumtuen. As it requires considerable extra effort to
follow the recommended route via the Rheiddol valley the author has
nominated Pontbren Plwca, the bridge over the Rheiddol at 727782 as
a checkpoint for achievement of his version of the Cambrian Way.

For the Rheiddol route leave Cwmystwyth by a gate opposite the
old school and follow the map closely on some ill-defined paths to Forestry Commission forest and thence to The Arch, a stone structure over
the Cwmystwyth to Devil's Bridge road built in 1810 to commemorate
George III's accession. A pleasant track commencing shortly to west of
the arch leads to Devil's Bridge avoiding the sometimes busy tourist
road.

Devil's Bridge (Pontarfrynach) is a somewhat congested tourist
honeypot at the end of a narrow gauge railway. It is nevertheless
worth a visit if only to see the three generations of bridges, one above
the other, the oldest being 900 years old. The splendour of the Mynach
Falls, which you have to pay to see, varies, of course, according to
the amount of water flowing. The footpath off the A4120 leads to the
railway track but do not cross it yet. Keep SW of line through wood,
then go along actual track for 200m before path down valley side to
footbridge called Pontbren Plwca (check point 18). This superb spot,
with waterfalls and the beautiful Rheidol valley around, was once
marred by the Cwm Rheidol lead mine, relics of which are passed on the
path up to Ystumtuen. See Youth Hostel section for information about
Ystumtuen. The route continues to Dyffryn Castell using a short
stretch of the A44 at Ponterwyd and passing a post office/shop. An
alternative is to follow a waymarked route to Parson's Bridge, a footbridge over a really dramatic and deep gorge, but the rest of the way
involves 2½ miles of road walking.

Dyffryn Castell to Dylife via Plynlimon (Punlumon)   11½ miles
2560 feet of ascent   Maps 30 & 31

The approach to Plynlimon from Dyffryn Castell is long and relatively little used compared to the shorter route from Eisteddfa Gurig.
Much of the way is undefined and in cloud a compass will be necessary
until the fence is reached, after which one is by a fence almost to the
summit. There one will find a ring of stones in which many walkers
have sought some shelter from wind and rain. Here on the main summit

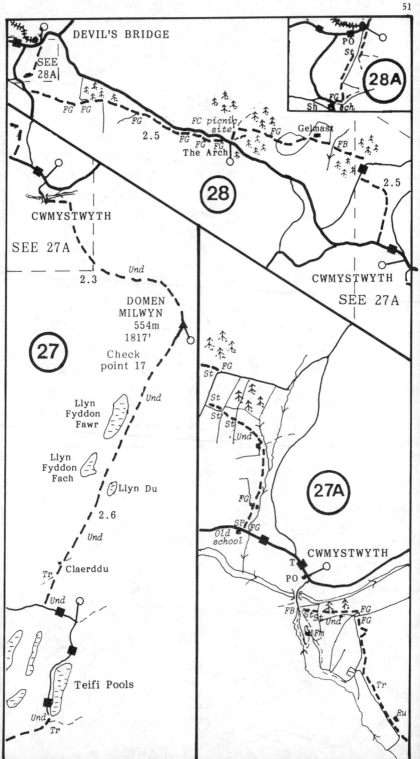

DEVIL'S BRIDGE

SEE 28A

FG FG

FG

2.5

FC picnic site

FG FG FG

The Arch

Gelmast

FG

FB

2.5

28

CWMYSTWYTH

SEE 27A

2.3

Und

DOMEN MILWYN
554m
1817'
Check point 17

27

Llyn Fyddon Fawr

Und

Llyn Fyddon Fach

Llyn Du

2.6

Und

Tr Claerddu

Und

Teifi Pools

Und

Tr

CWMYSTWYTH

SEE 27A

FG

St

St

St

St

Und

FG

SP FG

Old school

27A

CWMYSTWYTH

T

PO

FB St St Und FG FG

Fm

Tr

Ru

PO
St

28A

FG
Sh Sch

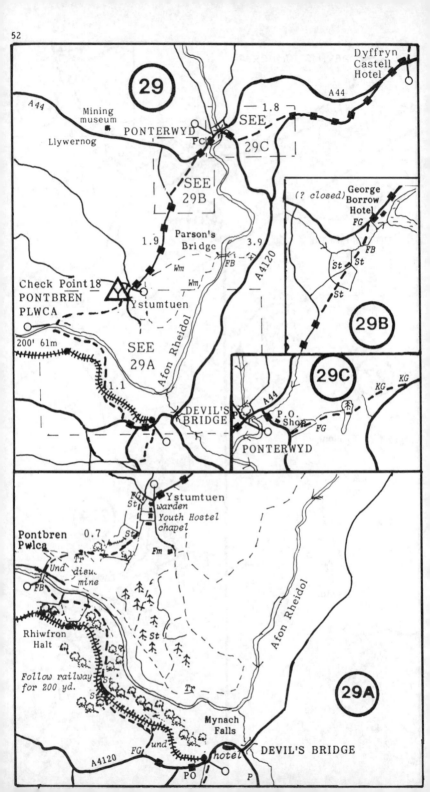

of Plynlimon one can feel one is at the heart of Central Wales, in the middle of a vast area of moorland, at times worthy of the cynics title of "sodden weariness" but generally in summer good walking terrain.

Plynlimon is Crown common with a legal right of public access (see page 14) but this right was under threat recently due to a misguided scheme of the Crown Estate Commissioners, following buying up of the last remaining commoner, to fence off certain areas to provide shelter belts for tree planting and to improve other areas. The scheme was to be in commemoration of the marriage of the Prince and Princess of Wales but this gesture was not at all appreciated by the Countryside Commission or any of the amenity bodies such as the Ramblers' Association, Council for the Protection of Rural Wales and the Youth Hostels Association. They were particularly incensed that the Crown Estate erected a long barbed wire fence before the Secretary of State for the Environment had had a chance to decide if it was for the "benefit of the neighbourhood". In the event the Secretary of State settled for a compromise so that no new fences will appear near the summit but the prematurely erected fence (not seen from Cambrian Way) will have periodic stiles in it.

The Machynlleth Variant. The summit of Plynlimon is a possible junction for beeliners determined to get to Cader Idris via Machynlleth. This saves 16½ miles compared with the recommended route. There is a fine route on rights of way via Hyddgen, the escarpment of Creigiau Bwlch Hyddgen and passing east of Glanmerin Lake to Machynlleth. This busy little market town may prove an attraction with its better supplies than those available from the village post offices recently encountered. Looking ahead on the route in this guide one can expect good grocery shops at Mallwyd/Dinas Mawddwy and then not until Barmouth. Beyond Machynlleth there are routes into a much forested area but no right of way into the Talyllyn valley to the S.E. of Cader Idris between the way to Abergynolwyn via Foel y Geifr and the footpath to Bwlch Lynn Bach from Cwm Ratgoed except the A487 from Corris. The Abergynolwyn approach to Cader Idris is long and involving a repeat of the top section on the descent, and is not nearly such a good way up as the two offered in this guide. The road route from Corris is preceeded by more road walking from Machynlleth, although the Centre for Alternative Technology can be visited on the way. It is because of these problems but rather more the scenic qualities and interest of the route via Dylife, Mynydd Cemmaes, Dinas Mawddwy and the Maesglasau ridge that the connoisseur is advised to stick to the route in this guide.

Plynlimon has several summits and several sources of famous rivers. The Wye source lies a mile away to the east but more on the route is the source of the Severn. Do not be deceived however by the mobile post indicating the source of the Severn which moves around the boggy area whence floweth the longest river in the British Isles. Go north and cross the valley to hit the track leading round a headland to bring Lake Bugeilyn into view. Follow the bridleway between the two parts of the lake and at the ruins of the Bugeilyn farm cross the stream and go over the bank on an undefined public footpath. Watch for the site of an old reservoir which served the disused mine beyond. Follow the map into Dylife.

Glyndwr's Way. Half a mile before Dylife there is a crossing with a long distance footpath route devised and waymarked by Powys County Council. Glyndwr's Way is in two sections, each crossing from the Welsh coast near Machynlleth to the Offa's Dyke Path along the border with England. This is the southern section to Knighton. The northern section to Welshpool will be crossed near Commins Coch.

Glyndwr's Way traverses quiet and attractive Welsh countryside but 36 of its 120 miles are along tarred roads, i.e. 30% compared to 11% for Cambrian Way. In particular, it currently follows 3 miles of the busy A489 from Machynlleth. Unless dramatically improved, properly waymarked, and many new rights of way created, it is difficult to see how this route will justify the future national trail status that is currently favoured for it by the Countryside Commission.

31A

Dylife Star Inn

T +

site of lead works

old shafts

FG

N

DYLIFE

SEE 31A

Check Point 20

Penycrocben

2.8

FB

old reservoir

Und

Bugeilyn

31

Tr

Und

Carnfach-bugeilyn

Carn Fawr

Source of River Severn

Und

5.1

approx line of fencing

Und

N

PLYNLIMON
Check Point 19

Und

3.5

Eisteddfa Gurig

Und

Pen Pumlumon Arwystli

Und

Source of River Wye

Und

30

N

Und

approx line of fencing

Plynlimon ▲ 752m 2468'

Dyffryn Castell

Dylife. It is hard to believe that this quiet hamlet, 1200 feet up in the hills, with only a few houses and a pub, was, just over a century ago, the scene of intense mining activity. At that time vast quantities of lead were being mined, also copper and zinc, and many hundreds of miners were employed. The Romans almost certainly mined here and there was a fortlet on Penycrocbren, the hill to the south. It is a ghostly place with bare areas where the mine buildings have been removed and a churchyard with tombstones but no church left. The derelict barrack buildings are a reminder of the overcrowding that went on here with one bed shared by two miners who each did a 12-hour shift, and got into the warm bed left by the other. Pencrocbren (meaning gallows hill) has a gruesome tale to tell of a blacksmith at the mine who murdered his wife and daughter and threw their bodies down a disused shaft. At that time it was the custom to hang murderers near the scene of their crime and for the body to hang in a metal cage. His last job was to make his own cage, which is still preserved, at St. Fagans Folk museum at Cardiff.

The Star Inn is partly very old, with modern additions for a restaurant and bedrooms. If time permits a stroll should be made down the road from the village until the magnificent view down into the Pennant valley is obtained with the crags on the left and the waterfall of Ffrwd Fawr. For further reading see "Dylife" written and published by David Bick, Pound House, Newent, Glos. (1985 edition £2.10 post free).

Dylife to Commins Coch   8½ miles   750 feet of ascent   Map 32
                                                                        (& 32A & B).

The next section of the Cambrian Way is in complete contrast to the starkness of Plynlimon. It is a fascinating, undulating walk over two attractive passes, with a mixture of rough and improved grassland, forest and heather moorland. The whole route is shown at 1:25,000 scale as well as 1:50,000 because many field boundaries have to be crossed and it is necessary to have a map showing boundaries if one is not to stray from the public rights of way. Farmers in this section, and the next, will not be so used to seeing walkers as on most sections of the Cambrian Way, and it is important to establish good relations from the start. They may not even be too sure where the rights of way are judging by the absence of gates where there should be in some of the fences. Such cases have been reported to Powys County Council.

In the woods west of Esgair Geulan follow the roads and paths as shown on the map. Part of the right of way was planted on but a legal diversion between 848975 and 849979 became operative in July 1984, and has been waymarked. At Maesteg the Forestry Commission allows the use of the forest road but watch for the public footpath which turns sharply down at a bend in the forest road. (See pages 9 and 14.)

Commins Coch is a small village with a post office/shop but no pub or B.&B. at the time of writing. Trains pass through but do not stop nearer than Machynlleth to the west and Caersws to the east. (What about a Dales Rail scheme for this line?) There is a pleasant spot for a picnic on common land alongside the rushing river Twymyn to the south-east of the village at 849029. If B.&B. is needed it is best to push on to Cemmaes on the diversion shown on the sketch map, and return by minor road and bridleways to a point just north of the wood at 862057.

Commins Coch to Dinas Mawddwy   13 miles
        2460 feet of ascent   Map 33

Mynydd y Cemais is a broad ridge at about the 1300 foot contour which few people come to Wales to walk but which provides an exhilerating excursion with fine views of Cader Idris and the Aran mountains. It is moorland grazing land with numerous fences. Fortunately there is a reasonable network of public paths along it, though not always exactly where they would be most convenient. However a route entirely on public rights of way is suggested and should be kept to for reasons mentioned in the last section, even though this means a somewhat zig-zag route at Waun Llinau.

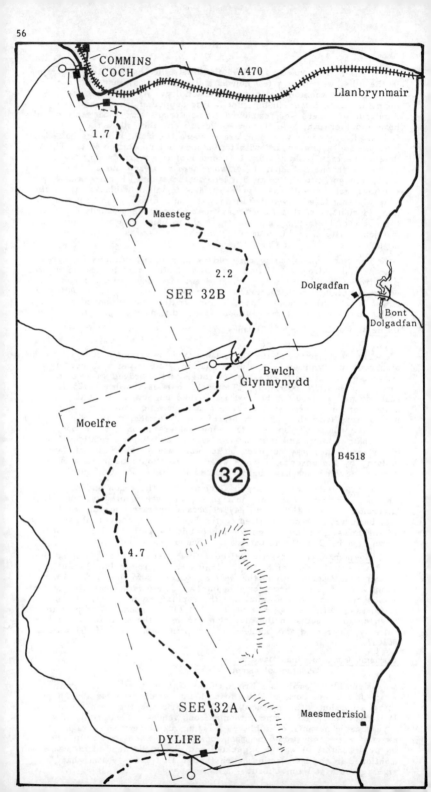

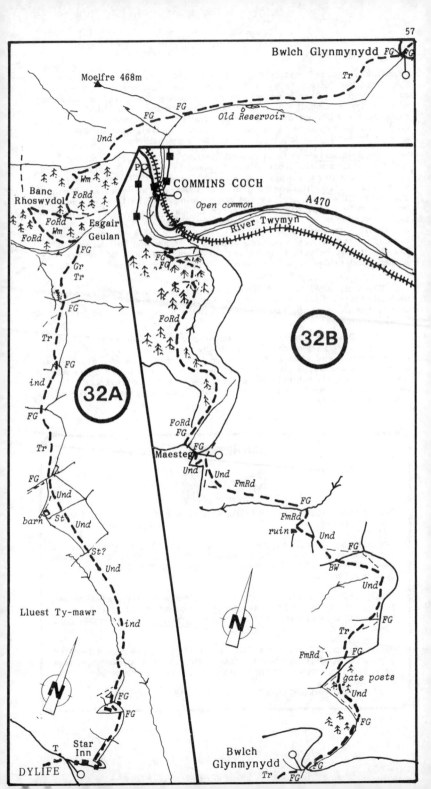

From higher ground east of Esgair Ddu an old track winds down into the attractive Tafolog valley with disused farm buildings at Craig-for and Bryn-glas. Thence grassy tracks and stony roads lead to Mallwyd, where there is a small supermarket and the Brigands Inn, which has a restaurant licence but does not serve drinks without meals. The minor road suggested to Dinas Mawddwy passes a delectable spot by the Dovey at Pont Mallwyd, and is preferable to the busy main road.

Dinas Mawddwy with its majestic setting at the junction of the Dovey and Cerist rivers will prove a worthy place to stay for the sheer beauty of its surroundings. Dinas Mawddwy was once noted for the lawlessness of its red headed brigands, but in later times was an important borough and market town. A century ago slate mining was the thriving industry but the railway that was built to serve it closed in 1951. The former railway station is now a cafe attached to the Meirion Mill woollen and craft enterprise with retail shop. There you can buy a fascinating and concise booklet on the history of Dinas Mawddwy. Before leaving the area of the old station be sure to lean over the downstream side of the now by-passed road bridge to see an even older packhorse bridge across the gorge.

The camp site, Celyn Brithion, has a superb panoramic spot for backpackers on raised ground above the caravan section. The Red Lion is the older of the two inns and Welsh singing is assured late on Saturday nights.

From Dinas Mawddwy a side excursion can be made to the Arans. Although never part of the author's route for Cambrian Way, they are fine mountains and slightly higher than Cader Idris. A row over denial of access to the Arans has only been partially solved by an agreement for use of specific routes. If approaching from the south ascent and descent must be made to the head of Cwm Cywarch. Distance 12½ miles, 3000 feet of ascent.

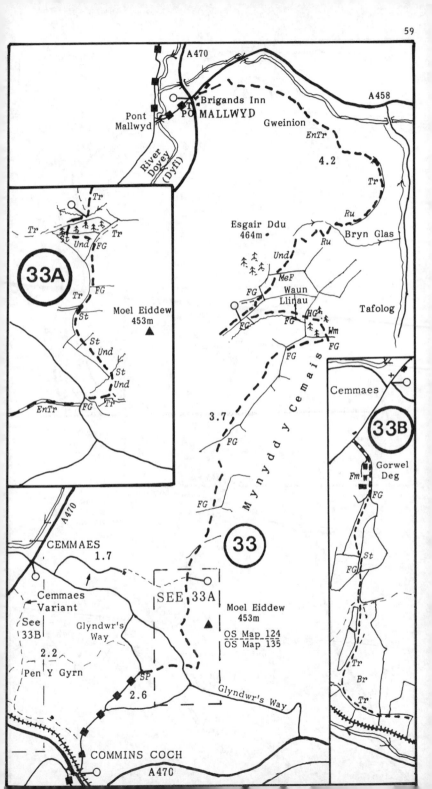

A470

A458

Brigands Inn
PO MALLWYD
Pont
Mallwyd
Gweinion
EnTr
4.2
River
Dovey
(Dyfi)

Tr

Ru

Esgair Ddu
464m
Ru
Bryn Glas

Tr
Tr
Tr
Und
St Und FG
Tr FG
Tr FG
St

FG
MeF
Waun
Llinau
HC
FG
FG
Wm
FG

Tafolog

33A

Moel Eiddew
453m ▲

St
St Und
St Und
EnTr FG Tr

FG

FG

3.7

FG

Cemmaes
+

33B

Gorwel
Deg
Fm
FG

Mynydd y Cemais

33

St
FG

A470

CEMMAES
1.7

Cemmaes
Variant
See
33B

SEE 33A

Moel Eiddew
453m
▲
OS Map 124
OS Map 135

2.2
Pen Y Gyrn

Glyndwr's
Way

Tr
Br

SP
2.6

Glyndwr's Way

Tr

COMMINS COCH
A470

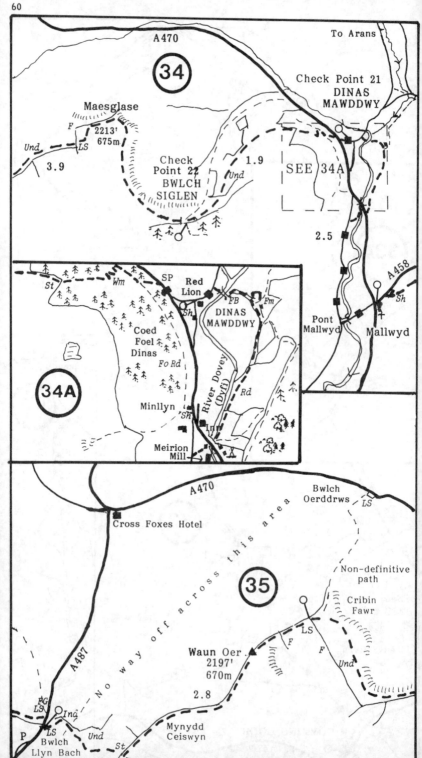

NORTHERN SECTION
DINAS MAWDDWY TO CONWY
Through Snowdonia National Park

Dinas Mawddy to Barmouth via Maesglasau and Cader Idris   20 miles
            5526 feet of ascent   Maps 34 to 38

The obliquely ascending path through the recently felled and re-
planted Coed Foel is obstructed above a forest road by a cliff face,
necessitating a detour along the forest road and then a steep climb
back to the line of the right of way. A diversion to legalise and
improve the detour was originally requested in 1979, but although a
zig-zag diversion was improved the legal process has been slow. Beyond the diversion the rough and gradually ascending path gets steeper
before emerging onto the open hillside at a corner of the moor. Hopefully this forest section will be waymarked.

From Bwlch Siglen to Mynydd Ceiswyn via Maesglasau and Waun Oer is
one of the finest sections of Cambrian Way with superb crag top walking
and wild moorland. This natural route across the mountains, already mentioned in several guides, is mostly clearly defined on the ground and a
short stretch is eroded in the steep dip between Cribin Fawr and Waun Oer.
A short peaty section on Cribin Fawr is best passed on the north side.

Bwlch Llyn Bach is presumably the name of the pass on the A487
despite its marking on the Ordnance maps on the opposite side of a
filled-in lake which gives its name to the pass (now a lay-by). Here a
decision has to be made as to alternatives. The main route makes the
approach to Cader Idris involving the least ascent. From a ladder stile
off the road on the north side of the pass, follow up a well worn path
by a fence for about a mile before a steeper scramble onto the broad main
ridge of the mountain. The alternative route, involving descent, partly
by old road, to the area of Minffordd and Lake Talyllyn, enables a night
to be spent there, if necessary, before making the most exciting approach to Cader Idris. This involves a steep wooded ascent followed by
a spectacular ridge climb up the enormous cwm surrounding Llyn Cau.

On the writer's first visit to Cader Idris a man in a little hut on the
summit dispensed cups of tea but there is no such hospitality there to-
day to greet the many who climb this deservedly popular mountain.
Perhaps more practically useful on occasions is the emergency shelter
just to the north of the summit.

It is tempting to descend by Fox's Path but this is very steep,
terribly eroded and strongly advised against. Much the better route is
westwards by gradual descent to the Pony Track at Rhiw Gwredydd,
thence north-east down a maintained path. Half way down, unless making for the national park car park, go left through gate, before bridle
gate on main path, and follow less used right of way down to the road.

Hostellers may make a beeline for Kings but they must also be
planning ahead and decide whether to press on to Barmouth. Few will
be capable of reaching Llanbedr and certainly not Ffestiniog along the
Cambrian Way route in one day from Kings. Maybe an easy 5½ mile
day to Barmouth with an indulgence in candyfloss and sea bathing is
called for before tackling the Rhinogs.

The walk to Barmouth through the lower foothills of Cader, past
the Cregennen Lakes and a waymarked path route, partly non-definitive,
leading down past Arthog waterfalls to the Mawddach estuary is a
fascinating walk. Lovers of walking old railway routes could, as an
alternative, follow the beautiful wooded valley down from Kings to the
estuary and then use the national park authority's railway path to Arthog.

Barmouth Bridge carries both the Cambrian Coast railway line and a
footbridge, for which there is a small toll. The future of the bridge and
of the whole line, not to mention Cambrian Way, was in some jeopardy in
1980 when it was thought the Teredo worm was destroying the bridge
timbers. However, the damage was not as bad as at first thought, but

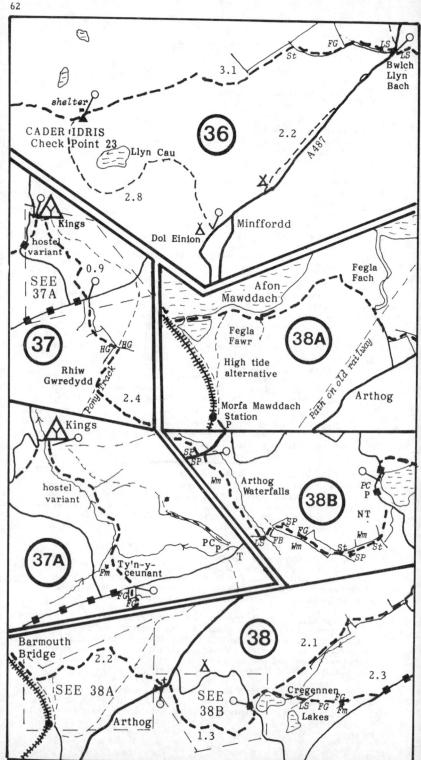

nevertheless, as the line is highly subsidised, there is an element of doubt about the bridge's future.

Barmouth to Maentwrog or Ffestiniog via the Rhinogs   22½ miles
7928 feet of Ascent   Maps 39 to 41

The Rhinog section of the Cambrian Way is at the same time the most demanding, the most rewarding and the most controversial part of the whole route. The traverse of the range should not be undertaken unless the walker is capable of moving safely over difficult terrain and capable of easy climbing with a pack on. Good navigational ability is essential and one must be prepared to take much longer than the distances suggest will be necessary.

Going is reasonably easy as far as the summit of Y Llethr the highest point in the range, but the central and northern sections involve much rock scrambling, often where heather obscures the boulders below. Avoiding short rocky climbs and descents will involve time wasting detours. Lone walkers particularly must appreciate the dangers of a sprained ankle or other accident in places where no one will hear or see them. The local volunteer mountain rescue organisation was very apprehensive of the creation of the Cambrian Way, not least because of the difficulty of finding an injured person amongst the rocks.

Very few walkers will be capable of doing the whole range in one day and many will find even half the way more than enough for one day. The backpacker scores on this part of the route in being able to stay in the mountains though a dry and rock free spot may be difficult to find in some parts. Those who want a roof over their head will find there is no accommodation near either Cwm Nantcol or Cwm Bychan. Lamentably Gerddi Bluog youth hostel has closed. This was two miles west of Cwm Bychan in a superb situation. Its purchase was subsidised by the Countryside Commission partly with the Cambrian Way in mind, but alas not enough hostellers would take the trouble to get to it, the Cambrian Way project foundered as an official path and the first edition of this guidebook came too late.

Stage planning for the normal distance walker, if not camping, or being car assisted from road heads at Cwm Nantcol or Cwm Bychan, is likely to involve a detour to Llanbedr or Harlech. The stage planning chart gives distances involved for a taxi assisted detour and return. Descent is made from the route at Bwlch Drws Ardudwy and Cwm Nantcol followed to Llanbedr or a taxi phoned for from the call box at 623262. Return next day by taxi could be to Maes-y-Garnedd. (See accommodation list for taxi details.)

Barmouth is a fascinating seaside resort sandwiched between the cliffs and either the sea or the Mawddach estuary. Depart by a path which starts as a steep flight of steps alongside an enormous gash of an old quarry. Note particularly the short zig zag further up the path. There is no way across the high walls between Gellfawr and Bwlch y Llan, so that a short walk down a minor road is necessary to a stile at 622166, whence an undefined path, with misleading waymarking at first, leads near to masts of a radio station, then up to Bwlch y Llan.

By negotiation with the owners the Snowdonia National Park has been able to open up a permissive route northwards from Bwlch y Llan by putting ladder stiles over the many substantial stone walls which previously prevented walking along this superb mountain ridge. The action of the owners is much appreciated but it should be noted that to emphasise that the route is not a public right of way, it is closed on February 5th each year. February is an unlikely and highly dangerous time of year to make an expedition along the Cambrian Way, but as a route had been surveyed before the new route was known about, a "February 5th Way" is shown on the south-east side of the ridge following public footpaths and an untarred county road to rejoin the ridgeline at the ancient pass north of Llawlech.

The de facto access route along the central Rhinog skyline has already featured in other guides notably "Classic Walks". For most of the

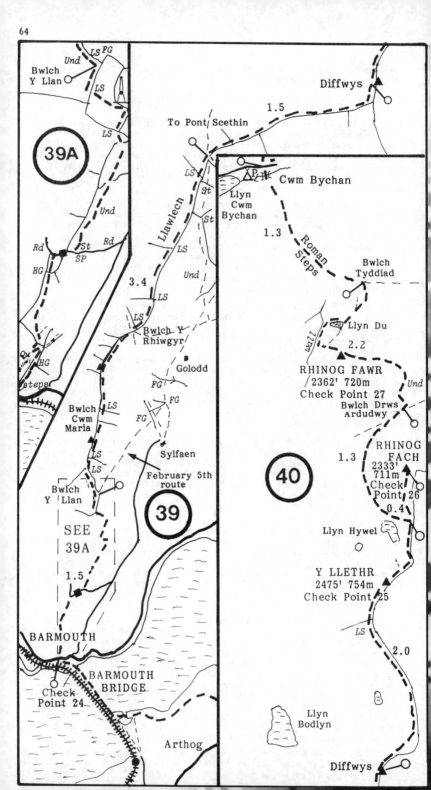

next section a path is visible on the ground. Further north the way is so rocky that no path is visible. There is a ladder stile across the only fence encountered.

Exhilerating ridge walking along Crib-y-rhiw leads to Y Llethr the highest point on the range. Beyond the summit keep to the end of the plateau and descend down a gully. Do not be tempted by a much eroded steep descent which leads more directly to Llyn Hywel. Rhinog Fach is suggested as a spur route using the scramble up the south end and same route for return to avoid steep and erosion prone descents elsewhere off the mountain.

Rhinog Fawr is, next to Tryfan, probably the rockiest mountain in Wales. Geologically and ecologically, however, it is very different, which is no doubt partly why the Nature Conservancy acquired it. Do not be deceived by the wide gradually ascending ledges as seen from the south side, but start scrambling up from near the actual pass of Bwlch Drws Ardudwy and take a wide sweep right to join the path up the east ridge. Descent north-westwards is eroded but unavoidable. Avoid direct descent to Llyn Du and make for wall, then follow wall and north side of lake. North-east from lake path leads round to Bwlch Tyddiad but avoid spurious path to left which would take you too high.

The so-called Roman Steps are now agreed as being of later origin. The ready supply of large boulders were used to make a packhorse route over these inhospitable mountains. They now provide thousands of tourists much pleasure and Cambrian Way walkers welcome faster progress than may have been experienced on the Rhinogs. The national park has carried out much improvement to the Steps path with the assistance of working parties of the B.T.C.V. An alternative to the Steps path is to press on along the main ridge via Craig Wion, but the going is very slow and probably not worth the saving of height against the drop to Cwm Bychan.

Cwm Bychan is a grand spot surrounded by rocky mountains and with a most attractive lake. The camp site has no facilities and is seldom crowded in consequence, but this may change if public toilets are erected to cater for the many who park there by day.

The northern Rhinogs are more rocky but less heathery than the central section. From just north of Clip to just west of Moel y Gyrafolen (534m) de facto access changes to de jure access because it is Crown common with a public right of access. A steep scramble from just before Bwlch Gwylim is probably the easiest way up to Clip, but it is undefined. Thence follows a remarkable walk, mostly along a bare rock plateau, interspersed with chasms that have to be climbed down and up again. Easy climbing is needed up a rock face but can be circumvented round the sides if necessary. Two small lakes should be identified for help in navigation, especially if the area is in cloud. In contrast Moel Ysgyfarnogod is a grassy mound followed by another dip and cliff to the even flatter rock plateau of Diffwys (not to be confused with the Diffwys at the southern end of the Rhinogs). It is important to come off the open land by the public footpath at the hunting gate at 674358 to the north of Moel y Gyrafolen. Any other ways in that area would involve climbing over walls, something our Connoisseur neve does.

At the minor road at Moelfryn main route walkers will go north by the signposted and waymarked path to the Trawsfynydd dam and down to Maentwrog. Hostellers making for Ffestiniog have a choice as to which way they go round Llyn Trawsfynydd. The distance is the same either way. The way round the west and north sides enables one to assess whether Sir Basil Spence and Sylvia Crowe made a good job of designing the nuclear power station, whilst if it is desired to keep as far away as possible from anything nuclear and if a cup of tea at Trawsfynydd is a consideration then the south and eastern route should be taken. The lake was made to supply hydro electric power in the 1930s and not for the nuclear power station.

The alternative hostel routes converge at a Roman amphitheatre,

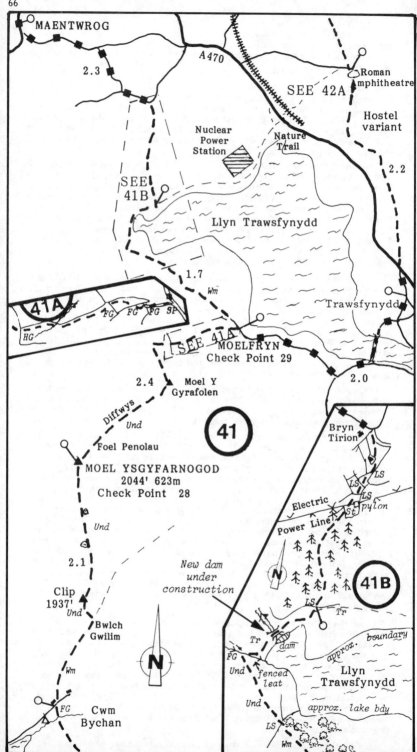

MAENTWROG

2.3

A 470

SEE 42A

Roman Amphitheatre

Hostel variant

2.2

Nuclear Power Station

Nature Trail

SEE 41B

Llyn Trawsfynydd

1.7

Wm

Trawsfynydd

41A

FG   FG   FG   SP

HG

SEE 41A

MOELFRYN
Check Point 29

2.0

2.4   ▲ Moel Y Gyrafolen

Diffwys

Und

Foel Penolau

41

Bryn Tirion

LS

LS

LS

MOEL YSGYFARNOGOD
2044' 623m
Check Point 28

Electric

St pylon

Power Line

Und

Und

2.1

Clip
1937'

Und

Bwlch Gwilim

Wm

FG

Cwm Bychan

New dam under construction

LS

Tr

41B

Tr

FG

Und   dam

fenced leat

approx. boundary

Llyn Trawsfynydd

approx. lake bdy

Und

LS

Wm

N

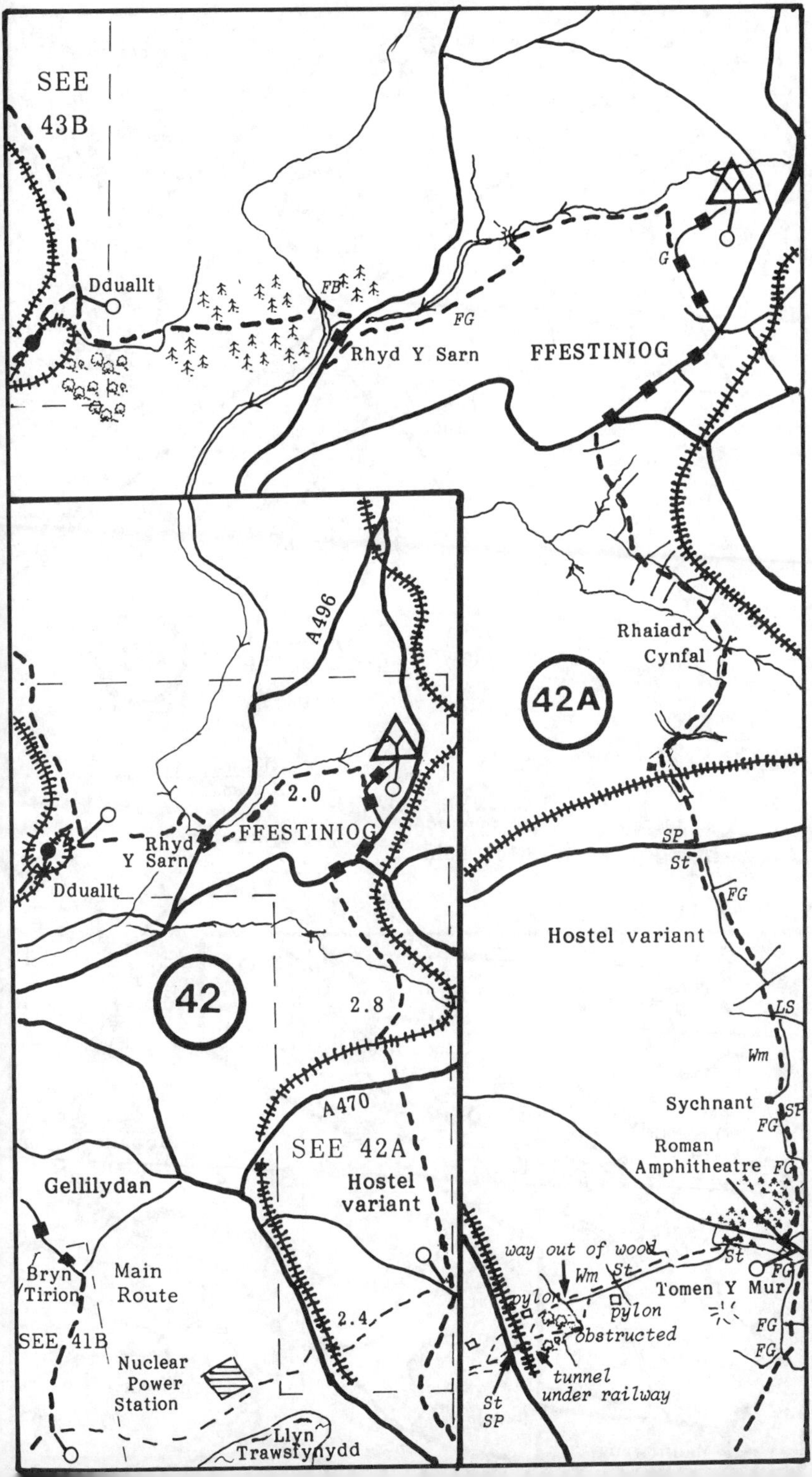

SEE
43B

Dduallt

FB

FG

Rhyd Y Sarn   FFESTINIOG

G

A496

2.0

Rhyd
Y Sarn   FFESTINIOG

Dduallt

42

A470

SEE 42A
Hostel
variant

Gellilydan

Bryn
Tirion   Main
Route

SEE 41B

Nuclear
Power
Station

Llyn
Trawsfynydd

42A

Rhaiadr
Cynfal

SP
St

FG

Hostel variant

LS

Wm

Sychnant   SP

FG

Roman
Amphitheatre   FG

way out of wood

Wm   St

pylon   St

pylon   FG

obstructed   Tomen Y Mur

FG

tunnel
under railway   FG

St
SP

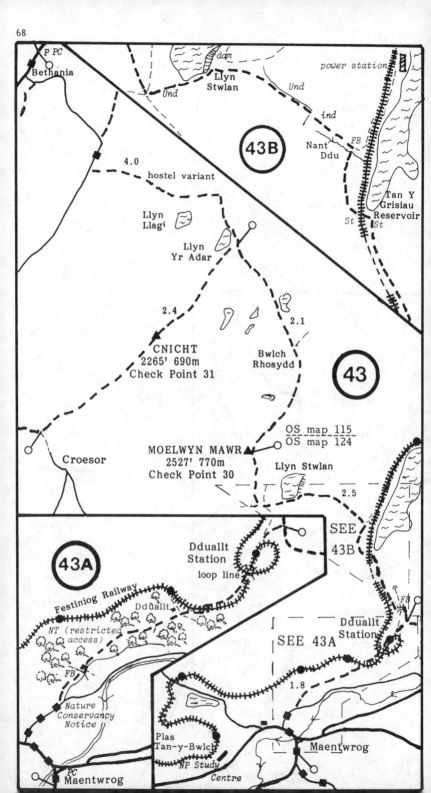

now only grassy mounds, with nearby Tomen-y-mur, a Roman fort
which Richard Sale describes as "the very frontier of the Empire with
pouring rain and pagan savages for company". Waymarked paths lead
on to Ffestiniog.

Maentwrog or Ffestiniog to Beddgelert or Bryn Gwynant
via Moelwyn Mawr and Cnicht   12.8 miles 3617 feet of ascent
(YH 10.6 miles 3387 feet of ascent)
Maps 42-44.

From Maentwrog a path leads through beautiful woods forming part
of the Coed Maentwrog national nature reserve. The National Trust
allows restricted access and one is asked to keep to the paths. Our
particular path leads round the lower side of a house called Bronturnor-
uchaf, and thence up to a crossing of the Festiniog railway, which is
crossed again at Dduallt station. Due to submergence of part of the disused line when the Tan-y-grisiau reservoir was made, the enterprising
organisation seeking to reopen this unique narrow gauge railway had to
make a new route at a higher level, involving a new tunnel and the
loop under which you pass before reaching the station. The train
could be used by Cambrian Way walkers seeking bed and breakfast in
Portmadoc or Blaenau Ffestiniog. Beyond the station the path runs a
short distance away on the east side of the railway.

Hostellers staying at Ffestiniog descend by a cascading Afon
Teigl to Rhyd-y-sarn and then over the Afon Goedol and through a
conifer plantation to rejoin the main route below Dduallt station.

The right of way previously passing across the south end of
Tan-y-grisiau reservoir has been diverted to the west side of the railway and should be followed to a footbridge over Nant Ddu, before
striking up to Llyn Stwlan on a none too obvious footpath. At the
dam go round the south end.

Llyn Stwlan is the upper reservoir of a pump storage system.
Power from Trawsfynydd nuclear power station is used in the night to
pump water from Tan-y-grisiau reservoir up to Llyn Stwlan, then let
out to generate power at peak times. When rights of way were first
shown on O.S. maps the path was shown going through the lake, but
later editions have not shown it at all. At this point and for the way
up and down Moelwyn Mawr the question of following a right of way is
rather academic since there is public right of access because it is
either crown common or a common in the former urban district of
Ffestiniog.

Moelwyn Bach can also be climbed before Moelwyn Mawr, but its
north ridge is very steep and treacherous. As it does not fit in conveniently with our route it has not been included in the recommended
itinerary.

Moelwyn Mawr is a worthy summit with fine views (if clear of
course) of the Snowdon range, the coastline and the Rhinogs. Beneath
one is a mountain riddled with mines which have been used for the
storage of explosives. A few years ago there was a scare about whether
the explosives had deteriorated to an extent that there was a danger to
Llyn Stwlan's dam, and the lake was promptly emptied.

This is one of the wildest and most desolate sections of the Cambrian
Way and can be very inhospitable in rain and cloudy conditions. Good
map reading is particularly important here. From Moelwyn Mawr summit
descent is made to the gaunt ruins of the Rhosydd quarry buildings
and thence a faint path winds its way past small lakes to a point near
Llyn yr Adar, where a left turn is made to join Poucher's route to the
summit of Cnicht. ("The Welsh Peaks".)

At this point hostellers can retrace their steps to Llyn yr Adar and
follow the path down to a minor road and thence by footpath, partly
through forest, to Llyn Gwynant, and back a short distance on the main
road to the driveway to Bryn Gwynant hostel.

The main route continues down the steep south-west ridge of
Cnicht. Great care is needed for a short section where the best way is

a short climb down on rock on the right hand side of the ridge. The gradient eases off and the route continues as a courtesy path waymarked by the national park, and is slightly different to Poucher's earlier editions in that it comes off the mountain at the pass on the Croesor to Nantmor track and not at Croesor village itself. A look back to Cnicht shows it as quite an imposing mountain, but it is really an insult to the most famous mountain in the Alps to call it the "Welsh Matterhorn".

Due to an inconsistency between the definitive maps of the old Merioneth and Caernarfon counties, the old road crossing the former county boundary at 623452 is shown in different ways but it is a public highway down to Bwlchgwernog. A minor road is followed to Nantmor and a footpath to Pont Aberglaslyn. The old railway tunnel, now part of a circular walk from the national park car park at Nantmor, may be tempting, but nothing should deter our Connoisseur from viewing the spectacular cascade at Aberglaslyn Pass, as seen from the road bridge and more particularly from the exciting path alongside the river. The river path ascends to the old railway track, just beyond the north end of the tunnel. Rejected plans to reopen the Welsh Highland railway would have affected the fine walk along the old track. Where the railway crossed the river the old bridge can be used to cross sides of the river to visit the grave of Gelert, the faithful dog of Llywelyn the Great (see Richard Sale's book), but the more pleasant route is to keep on the east side into Beddgelert, and maybe pay homage to Gelert after refreshment.

Beddgelert to Pen-y-Pass via Snowdon   10 miles   3590 feet of ascent
Maps 44 & 45

Beddgelert is a deservedly popular tourist village, its main disadvantage being the traffic that pours through it and which in particular goes over the attractive bridge in the village centre. There are inns, shops, cafes and accommodation here. Considering that Beddgelert is only the same distance away from Snowdon summit as Llanberis, it has done little to develop a direct walking route to the country's highest mountain. To get to the so-called "Beddgelert Path" would involve a ghastly 2½ mile walk along the busy A4085 Caernarfon road. The original plans for Cambrian Way suggested the direct route via the ridge of Yr Aran, but the need to use rights of way wherever possible has led to a realisation that the Nant Gwynant approach alongside Llyn Dinas is so attractive that it is perhaps preferable anyway.

Hostellers from Bryn Gwynant come along the main road to join the main route at Pont Bethania, near the national park car park.

The Watkin Path is in many ways the most attractive approach to Snowdon, albeit the one involving the greatest ascent. The lower parts are on the track going to the old mines and quarries in Cwm Llan, and this has been skilfully restored in recent years by expert boulder movers as part of the Snowdon Management Scheme funded by the Countryside Commission.

The Watkin Path was opened by Gladstone in 1892, at the age of 84, during his fourth term of office as prime minister, the occasion being commemorated by a plaque on the Gladstone Rock. Supposedly Sir Edward Watkin had the path above the quarries made to the summit by a route to take in the view of the Snowdon Horseshoe but no account was taken of the impracticability of maintaining a good path across the very unstable south flank of Snowdon summit. Although large sums of money   have been allocated to Snowdon's paths, the upper part of the Watkin Path remains an unsolved and most intractable erosion problem. Fortunately however for Cambrian Way, there is no need to go that way at all as there is a better way up Allt Maenderyn and Bwlch Main ridge.

Just after passing some waterfalls and before the ruin of the mine manager's house, at 621520, an unsigned public footpath goes sharply left up an incline. After 300 yards turn right onto the line of an old tramway and follow this for about another 300 yards, then strike half left towards the pass of Bwlch Cwm Llan. The line of the right of way

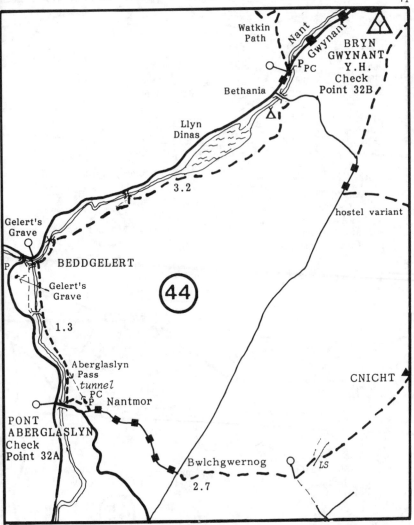

is only vaguely discernible and peters out altogether nearer the pass.
Once on Allt Maenderyn the way is up a broad rocky ridge. Some
sections are getting eroded, mostly by those dashing down this ridge,
but our Connoisseur, being on the ascent will add little to the erosion.
The ridge is broad enough for the eroded parts to be bypassed but do
not just walk on the edge of the erosion - that's the next bit to go.
Walk well away from the worn route - if all use was spread out the grass
cover would not be damaged. Higher up the ridge narrows, particularly
after being joined by the Llechog ridge and the route is slightly airy
before the final scramble to the summit.

Snowdon summit will, more likely than not, be in cloud, even if
the rest of the way up has been clear. Chris Jesty in his admirable
panorama guide to Snowdon summit, reckons that the odds against seeing the nearby peak of Lliwedd as 1.1 to 1, with 400 to 1 against
seeing Scafell Pike, the highest point in England.

The summit receives about 200 inches of rain and many hundreds
of thousands of visitors a year. If you had ideas of celebrating reaching
the climax point of the Cambrian Way by sitting admiring the view with

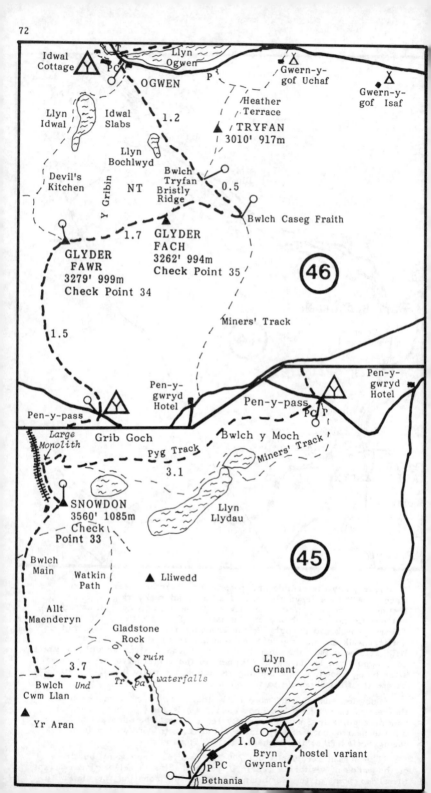

a pint of beer, at a table on a terrace at the cafe, then dispel this idea quickly. There may be so many in the cafe that you refuse to wait to be served, there are no terraces with tables, and the cafe may be closed. It is only open when the railway is running, and does not open until some time after Easter because of snow in the railway cuttings. You are in a "dry" county of Wales and will not be served with beer on Sundays. Even a glass of water may be a problem as it all has to be brought up in the train.

Any soil that there once was near the summit pyramid has gone and serious suggestions have been made for people to be asked to carry small bags of earth up with them. The surroundings of the cafe and station are such that Prince Charles is said to have remarked that this is the highest slum in Britain. There are plans for improvements but the costs of working at such a site are enormous.

Despite all the problems besetting Snowdon summit these do not alter the importance of Snowdon as the worthy climax of the Cambrian Way. It is a mountain on the grander scale than anything else en route and its magnificence is not belittled by its popularity.

From the summit area follow the path parallel to the railway to the enormous stone monolith at Bwlch Glas (spot height 993m) put up to indicate the vital point at which to hit the top of the Pyg or Pig Track. There is uncertainty as to whether the name of this famous path is derived from an abbreviation of the Pen-y-gwyrd Hotel beyond the end of the path or from the Welsh word "moch", sometimes meaning pig, in the title of the pass called Bwlch Moch part way up the path. At the monolith a decision must be made whether to follow the Pyg Track down or whether to take the more exciting but very exposed Crib Goch ridge route to Bwlch Moch. This classic part of the Snowdon Horseshoe route is strongly advised against if carrying a heavy pack, or if the walker is not very sure footed or if there are bad weather conditions. The ridge is really very knife-edged and quite sheer for hundreds of feet either side.

The Pyg Track has carried many millions intent on reaching the highest point in England and Wales under their own steam. It is only in recent years that it has been fully appreciated that such usage on such terrain requires maintenance to prevent the path becoming most unpleasant and dangerous to walk. This path is where most effort has been expended but the cost has been considerably reduced by the use of volunteers from several organisations notably the British Trust for Conservation Volunteers. You may meet some of them working on the path, and if the idea of such public spirited work appeals to you, not necessarily on such arduous projects, have a word with them and write to B.T.C.V. at 35 St. Mary's Street, Wallingford, Oxon. for details of their national and local tasks.

The first section below the pass is appropriately called the Zig Zags and has been much improved. Do not be tempted to short cut - this is what caused such terrible erosion in the past. Further on there is another option, this time to descend to the Miners Track that runs up to the old mines by Llyn Glaslyn. This follows a wider path, crosses Llyn Llydaw by a causeway, and a much improved track to Pen-y-Pass. The Pyg track keeps higher up and crosses into the Llanberis valley at Bwlch Moch at the end of the Crib Goch ridge.

Pen-y-Pass, popular because at 1168 feet (356m) it is the highest road pass from which to climb Snowdon, consists of a youth hostel, restaurant and car park. Much to the disgust of many of the climbing fraternity the old Gorswyddfa Hotel at the pass was converted and extended, with large government grants, to become a very well appointed youth hostel. On the opposite side of the road is a large restaurant. If your mode of walking Cambrian Way involves the use of the car park, note that it is expensive and strictly limited in size. There is nowhere else to park legally near the pass. The Snowdon Sherpa bus service calls here but check on times with the Snowdonia national park office, tel. Penrhyndeudraeth 770274. It is possible to use the buses so as to spend a second night in Nant Gwynant and return to resume the walk at Pen-y-Pass, thus allowing a light rucksack for Snowdon.

Pen-y-Pass to Ogwen via the Glyders   4.8 miles   2353 feet of ascent
Map 46.

The path leading onto the Glyders is over a ladder stile on the Llanberis side of the hostel building. You then enter land owned by Mrs. Esme Kirby, of Dyffryn Mymbyr, near Capel Curig. She has been sheep farming this side of the Glyder range since the 1930s, when her former husband Thomas Firbank wrote the best selling book "I Bought a Mountain". The book is well worth reading, particularly for its insight into the problems of sheep farming in the wilder parts of Wales. Esme is now the chairman and driving force of the Snowdonia National Park Society.

There is no defined path for most of the way up the broad south ridge of Glyder Fawr, and compass and good map reading will be necessary in cloud. Assuming that the Ogwen valley is to be a staging point before the long trek over the Carneddau, our Connoisseur is advised either to have a short day from Pen-y-Pass to Ogwen or to get to Ogwen early enough to make separate sorties in this superb mountain area to, say, Tryfan or Cwm Idwal. By making Glyder Fach a checkpoint as well as Glyder Fawr use will be discouraged of the eroded descent from Glyder Fawr to Llyn Cwm and the frustrating boulder descent below the Devil's Kitchen. From Glyder Fach there are several possible descents, such as the Gribin or the very airy Bristly Ridge, but the recommended safe way is to proceed further east along the Glyder plateau to Bwlch Caseg Fraith, where the Miner's Track from Pen-y-Gwryd to Ogwen crosses over.

Tryfan, as the rockiest mountain in Wales is ideal for learning to climb (and the author has happy memories of the easier climbs there), but the north ridge is not for the uninitiated to descend with a large rucksack and therefore Tryfan has not been made a Cambrian Way checkpoint. The traverse of Tryfan is however a splendid expedition, but best achieved from north to south. On the top (3010 ft.) there are two prominent boulders, Adam and Eve. A mountaineer's initiation is sometimes to jump from one to the other.

From Bwlch Tryfan the Miner's Track passes Llyn Bochlwyd, an attractive spot, or a rougher way down is by Heather Terrace on the east side of Tryfan.

Ogwen has probably the finest panorama of mountains around it of anywhere in Wales and maybe this was why it gave its name to a rural district of Caernarvonshire before local government reorganisation. Certainly it was not the population living at Ogwen which gave it importance, since the place consists only of a mountain school, a youth hostel, tea bar, toilets and small car park. There is no pub or B.&B. The National Trust owns virtually all the land you can see and does not allow camping except at the organised sites which are at Gwern Gof Isaf and Uchaf. This sounds a rather inhospitable place but it could be easily spoiled. Nearby at Cwm Idwal is a national nature reserve, and a pleasant evening stroll can be made from the hostel to follow the nature trail round Llyn Idwal, amidst the spellbinding scenery of the glacially carved valley.

Ogwen to Conwy via the Carneddau   18   miles   4697 feet of ascent
Maps 47 - 49

The final section of the Cambrian Way is longer than most other stages suggested but is not as long as the 28 mile final stretch of the Pennine Way. The journey can more easily be broken as there is a youth hostel about two-thirds of the way along. On the other hand, this section has other hazards which can have serious consequences since 4½ miles run at over 3000 feet. At that level the mountains are more often in cloud than not and just as much in summer as at any other time. Conditions of wind, rain and snow can be unbelievably treacherous.

48

Drum
2529'
771m

Roman road

Bwlch Y Ddeufaen

SEE 49A

Foel Fras
3091'
942m

Garnedd
Uchaf

3.0

2.7 *shelter*

Drum

Foel Grach

CARNEDD LLEWELYN
3485' 1062m
Check Point 38

2.7

CARNEDD DAFYDD
3423' 1044m
Check Point 37

47

3211'
979m
Penyrolewen

1.3

Check
Point 36

Talyllyn
Ogwen

1.1

Llyn
Ogwen

A5

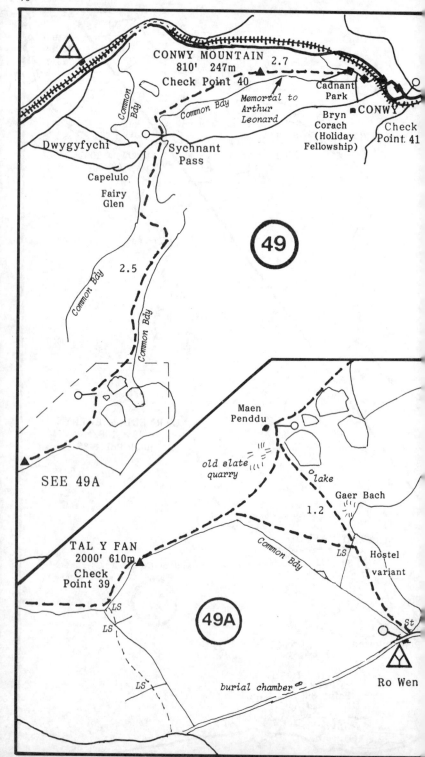

CONWY MOUNTAIN
810' 247m
Check Point 40

2.7

Memorial to
Arthur Leonard

Cadnant
Park

Bryn
Corach
(Holiday
Fellowship)

CONWY

Check
Point 41

Dwygyfychi

Sychnant
Pass

Capelulo

Fairy
Glen

2.5

49

SEE 49A

Maen
Penddu

old slate
quarry

lake

Gaer Bach

1.2

LS

Hostel
variant

TAL Y FAN
2000' 610m
Check
Point 39

Common Bdy

LS

St

LS
LS

49A

LS

burial chamber

Ro Wen

There are escape routes but these can leave the walker in remote valleys miles from anywhere. There seems to be no satisfactory low level alternative route. If bad weather prevails on the last day of a holiday and time does not permit an extra day discretion may be the better part of valour. On the other hand, navigation is not as difficult over the Carneddau as many parts of the Cambrian Way which may have already been traversed in cloud.

The whole way from Ogwen to Conwy is either National Trust land with unrestricted access (Ogwen to beyond Drum) or is over common land in former urban districts, some of it also crown common, and therefore with public right of access for air and exercise. Once over the stiles at Ogwen there are no more stiles or gates to negotiate on the main route.

Just over the road bridge at Ogwen go over the slate stile in the wall. This was put up in memory of Alfred Embleton, a youth hostel pioneer and for many years hon. treasurer of the Ramblers Association. The obvious route onto the Carneddau is straight up Penyrole-wen, average gradient 1 in 2½, but it has become frightfully eroded, unpleasant and dangerous, and is not recommended. Instead a longer and more pleasant way starts along the north side of Llyn Ogwen. The public footpath becomes undefined near Tal-y-llyn Ogwen Farm. Turn left before the river at the farm and proceed up, parallel to the river. Those who have stayed the night in the Gwern Y Gof area can join the route here by the public footpath through the farm. In order to discourage use of the eroded direct approach to Penyrole-wen this junction at Tal-y-llyn Ogwen is a checkpoint. Head for a ladder stile and then when due east of the prominent crags on the left make for an obvious gully where an easy scramble leads up to the east ridge of Penyrole-wen.

Most of the way along the Carneddau is on reasonably firm ground - no floundering in bog to get to a summit such as the Cheviot. Along the main ridge the way is usually visible on the ground though at places like above Craig Llugwy the rocky ground does not reveal any path, and the drop on the left needs to be kept in view. The ridge is mostly broad north of Carnedd Llewelyn but is generally cairned. A sharp turn at Garnedd Uchaf for no apparent reason on open plateau needs to be watched for. Once a fence looms up on the right about half a mile before Foel Fras navigational worries should be over for the next five miles as one follows the fence line all the way to beyond Tal-y-fan.

If making a detour to the delightful small hostel at Roewen, there are three options as to where to turn off the main route but one should bear in mind that Tal-y-fan is a check point.

From Tal-y-fan (just 2000 feet) the way is across open common, mostly on rights of way, but the most spectacular section is a nondefinitive traverse path on an ex urban district common leading to Sychnant Pass. The road crossing was once the main coast road before tunnels were made in the cliff at Penmaen-bach Point.

Positively the last climb is to the summit of Conwy Mountain, a worthy last peak with views this time of the sea as well as of the mountains behind. Gorse and heather in late summer make this a most pleasant spot. In your haste to reach Conwy Castle, now in sight, do not miss the memorial plaque to Arthur Leonard, the Congregational minister from Lancashire who introduced mill workers to the delights of walking in the Lake District and who later founded both the Cooperative Holidays Association (CHA) and later the Holiday Fellowship.

The castle at Conwy makes a fitting terminus for our long walk. Hope you have enjoyed it - you certainly won't forget it and my guess is that you will return to explore more of Wales you didn't know. You will find, as the author has done that the Welsh mountains grow on you. You will also wonder what all the fuss was about in the opposition to the Cambrian Way.

STAGE PLANNING SCHEDULE

This section seeks to assist in planning to walk the Cambrian Way. It will be noted that heights of ascent are given against all distances. This must be taken very seriously into account in estimating the time required for each daily section.

Naismith's formula of three miles per hour plus half an hour per thousand feet is reduced to about two and a half miles an hour plus three quarters of an hour per thousand feet for those carrying heavy packs. Slower walkers and leaders of parties (where inevitably the pace is that of the slowest), would be wiser to work on two miles per hour plus an hour per thousand feet.

Plan to finish well before sunset to allow for mistakes in navigation, fatigue and accidents, but as a precaution ensure that every member of a party has a torch that works, if only to read a map by when it is still possible to see one's way.

Distances in the chart below are derived from map measurements and are shown in miles with horizontal lines above and below them. The lines are level with the places between which the distances relate. The Y.H.A. and other variants columns show relevant distances and heights for some likely deviations from the main route.

The stages shown are not necessarily all suggested as daily sections and in some cases two or more sections may be covered in a day. More detailed distances are shown between flagged points on the 1:50,000 maps in this guide.

Cambrian Way is planned as a northbound excursion working up to a climax in Snowdonia. Do not be tempted to omit the Cardiff to Abergavenny section and then regret later on that the whole path has not been walked. It is well worth walking but do not try to "knock it off" in two days unless you are already very fit and are sure you can do it. Most people try to do too much in the early days of a long distance walk. After all, there's always Richard Sale's book on Cambrian Way to read in the evenings.

Main Route Cumul. Miles	Stage Miles	Feet of Ascent Northbound	Staging Points	Y.H.A. Variants Miles	Y.H.A. Variants Ascent	Other Variants Ml.	Other Variants Asc.
			SOUTHERN SECTION				
0			Cardiff Castle				
	5.4	125					
5.4			Tongwynlais				
	8.3	875					
13.7			Machen				
	3	1022					
16.7			Risca				
	8.2	1504					
24.9			Pontypool				
	11.3	1691					
36.2			Abergavenny	---		10.7	2885
	13.1	3443	Llanthony	14.2	3913		
49.3			Capel-y-ffin	---			
	16.0	2652		15.5	2347	11.6	2144
			Pengenffordd			10.2	2338
65.3			Crickhowell	---			
	13.2	2191					
78.5			Torpantau Pass	---			
	6.8	2705					
85.3			Storey Arms	8.5	2945	---	
			Llwyn-y-celyn Y.H.				
	8.1	2183	Ystradfellte Y.H.	7.3	1150	12.1	1470
			Glyntawe	17.3	4000	---	
93.4			A4067 Bwlch Bryn-rhudd	16.0	3000		
	7.2	1940	Llanddeusant Y.H.	---	---	7	2040
100.6			Llanddeusant - Trecastle Rd.			---	
	3.8	359	Myddfai	17.3	2500		
104.4							
	3.5	473	Llandovery				
107.9			Bryn Poeth Uchaf Y.H.	---			
	107.9	21163	Southern Section Sub-Totals				

Main Route Cumul. Miles	Stage Miles	Feet of Ascent North-bound	Staging Points	Y.H.A. Variants Miles	Y.H.A. Variants Ascent	Other Variants Ml.	Other Variants Asc.
			CENTRAL SECTION				
107.9	---		Llandovery	7.5	1483		
	6.6	1033	Bryn Poeth Uchaf Y.H.				
114.5	---		Rhandirmwyn	9.9	984		
	12.0	1579	Tyncornel Y.H.	---			
126.5	---		Mt. Rd. Nant y Maen	7.4	950	---	
	6.6	946	Blaencaron Y.H.	---		6.8	926
			Pontrhydfendigaid			---	
133.1	8.9	1408	Strata Florida	23.2	3944	10.5	1438
142	5.0	590	Cwmystwyth				
147			Devil's Bridge				
	5.5	1340	Ystumtuen Y.H.	---			
152.5	11.4	2560	Dyffryn Castell				
163.9	8.6	750	Dylife			---	
172.5			Commins Coch			11.0	1095
	13.0	2460	Cemmaes			12.2	2270
185.5	---		Dinas Mawddwy				
	77.6	12666	Central Section Sub-Totals				
			NORTHERN SECTION (Snowdonia National Park)				
185.5	8.6	2883	Dinas Mawddwy	---			
194.1			Bwlch Llyn Bach A487	15.0	5096	10.8	2883
			Minffordd			---	
	11.3	2643	Kings Y.H.	5.6	700	11.0	3048
205.4	---		Barmouth				
			Cwm Nantcol	16.7	4118	13.4	3882
	14.0	5534	(Phone box)				
			Llanbedr	---			
			Cwm Nantcol	4.4	580		
			(Maes y garnedd)	---		12.8	4230
219.4	8.5	2394	Cwm Bychan	15.7	4740		
227.9			Maentwrog			---	
	12.8	3617	Ffestiniog Y.H.	---			
240.7	---		Beddgelert	10.6	3387		
	10.0	3590	Bryn Gwynant Y.H.	7.8	3360		
250.7			Pen-y-pass	4.9	2353		
255.6	4.9	2353	Ogwen	13.5	---		
			Ro Wen Y.H.	17.1	4388		
	18.0	4697	Penmaenmawr Y.H.	6.4	---	909	
				4.2	809		
273.6	---		Conwy	---	---	---	
	88.1	27711	Northern Section Sub-Totals				
	273.6	61540	TOTALS - CAMBRIAN WAY				

MILES x 10

KILOMETRES
Miles 0.621 - 1 - 1.609 kilometres
METRES

FEET
Feet 3.281 - 1 - 0305 metres

MAPS FOR CAMBRIAN WAY

Maps are absolutely essential for navigation on the Cambrian Way. Most of the way is undefined on the ground and those used to the Pennine Way and most other long distance paths will find they have to be good map readers and that time must be allowed for frequent looks at the maps.

The maps in this guidebook are designed to be read in conjunction with the Ordnance Survey 1:50,000 Landranger maps and are not intended to be used on their own.

Map reading ability is essential to avoid unnecessary trespass and aggravation of farmers. Just a few bad map readers can incur the quite justifiable wrath of farmers if they climb over walls and fences where they have no right to go.

General Map. For planning purposes, sorting out one's travel to and from the area, and worth taking for identifying distant views is the Ordnance Survey's 1:250,000 Routemaster map, sheet 7, Wales and West Midlands, price £2.60 (1990). This map shows the mountain ranges clearly and marks railways and youth hostels.

1:50,000 (about $1\frac{1}{4}$ inch to mile) Landranger Series. Seven maps are required at £3.35 each (1990). The key maps on pages 16 and 17 give the key to these maps as well as to the strip maps in this guide. Note that there is an option between maps 146 and 147. Map 147 (Elan Valley and Builth Wells) is the map for walking the Elenydd - the wildest part of Wales, but it just omits Tregaron and part of its Bog, which comes on map 146. The weight of seven maps is $1\frac{1}{2}$lb (700 grams) but this can be reduced by removing the covers and cutting to about half or a third of area. See below re other advantages of such cutting. There is little advantage in buying the flat edition as the maps are more expensive. These maps show public rights of way but not field boundaries.

1:25,000 (about $2\frac{1}{2}$ inches to the mile). This scale is not necessary for following Cambrian Way as the inset maps in this guide show enough detail to facilitate navigation in the valley sections where field boundary information is important. If however, weight and cost considerations are not important, maps at this scale can enhance the enjoyment of the walk and ease navigation. The O.S. Leisure Map series covers the Snowdonia National Park sections of Cambrian Way on four maps. Cambrian Way traverses all three Leisure Maps of the Brecon Beacons National Park. The rest of the route is now covered by the Pathfinder series, of which 15 are required for complete coverage, together with the Leisure Maps just mentioned. The cost of the maps at this scale would be £68.79 (1990) and the weight $3\frac{1}{4}$ lbs. ($1\frac{1}{2}$ kilograms).

The Maps in this guide are of three kinds:-
1. Key maps - (a) South and (b) North, showing key to the 1:50,000 strip maps and to the 1:50,000 Ordnance Survey Landranger maps.

2. 1:50,000 strip maps covering the whole route, derived from out of copyright one inch to mile (1:63,360) Ordnance Survey maps of the 1920s, together with observed additions or amendments, and enlarged to 1:50,000 for convenience of readers' comparison with the current O.S. maps of that scale. They are serial numbered from the south end, with one, but sometimes two, maps on a page. North is at the top of the map unless otherwise marked.

3. Inset maps covering parts of the route, usually at 1:25,000 scale but some at six inch to mile (1:10,560) or other scales. These are derived from out of copyright six inch to the mile Ordnance Survey maps of about 1905. The scale has been contracted to 1:25,000 as being a scale familiar to walkers and one at which one can conveniently show field boundaries. Again all maps have north at the top unless otherwise marked. The maps are numbered with a letter following number of the 1:50,000 map of which they are an enlargement. Thus 25B is a second inset map relating to map 25.

Map Carrying

Particular attention needs to be paid to the problems of frequently referring to both the O.S. 1:50,000 maps and to the maps in this guide book. Mis-navigation is usually due to not looking at the maps often enough and this in turn is usually due to the physical difficulties of viewing them easily. It may be easy enough to refer to them if the weather is fine and the user has large cagoule pockets, but what if it is raining or blowing a gale? If it is too hot to wear a cagoule or jacket will the maps go in the pockets of one's lower garment?

Ideally one needs an arrangement whereby the two maps and the description can be viewed through the transparent plastic of a bag that can be folded up and the whole affair slipped into a hip pocket when not in use. This ideal is well nigh impossible without some compromise.

Map cases are usually about ten inches square and will take an O.S. map bent over as it is not meant to be to show two segments each side. Most map cases are too rigid to go in a pocket and have a cord so that they can be suspended round the neck. The author of this guide is one who detests such flapping cases and prefers to use 15"x20" "Seal again" plastic bags which will take an O.S. map with four segments showing one way, and without distorting the map from its normal folds. The bag is pliable enough to fold with the map and go in a pocket. Such bags can be supplied by Transatlantic Plastics, Ventnor, Isle of Wight (minimum 10 for £3.20 post free as at April 1985).

The compromise that can be made is to reduce the bulk of both the O.S. map and the guide book. For a start the covers of the map can be removed (there may be no covers anyway soon if plans for integral covers come to fruition) and the map cut in size. As regards this guide book, it has been arranged that the pages of route description and maps are in the centre of the book so that they can be removed by opening the staples. Thus only the map and description in use need be in the map carrier.

Pockets for maps can also be a problem. Walking and climbing breeches usually have good deep pockets with zip or button fastening but jeans and shorts usually have uselessly small pockets. It is worth considering sewing on a pocket on the inside front of the waistband.

WEATHER FORECASTS

Snowdonia National Park - updated 6a.m. or as necessary, Llanberis (0286 or local dialling code) 870120.

Commercial weather services at 25p per minute evenings and weekends, 38p per minute peak and standard times. Updated 6a.m. & 6p.m.

"Weatherdial" 0898 141 272 all Wales, 219 south Wales, 223 north and central Wales.

"Weathercall" 0898 500 then 740 or 409 Gwent & Glamorgan (S.Wales), 741 or 414 Dyfed & Powys (Central Wales), 742 or 415 Gwynedd & Clwyd (North Wales).

Cardiff Weather Centre, Cardiff (0222) 397020 for information about the weather services.

YOUTH HOSTEL SECTION

The Cambrian Way is blessed with a chain of Youth Hostels which is already more complete than was available on the Pennine Way when that Path was opened. Those who desire a roof over their heads at night will find it is almost essential to use hostels in some of the central Wales sections, and even in the heart of Snowdonia, there is only Youth Hostel accommodation at Pen-y-pass and Ogwen. At between a third and two thirds of the price of bed and breakfast establishments they provide at least basic needs and in some cases almost luxurious facilities, together with a friendly atmosphere and understanding of walkers' needs. The facility to make a meal quite late at night, and early in the morning gives hostellers much greater flexibility than staying in commercial accommodation. Whilst the higher grade and larger hostels have greater facilities and comfort, some veteran hostellers may find the exuberance of large parties of youngsters somewhat wearing. They may find the smaller simpler hostels in south and central Wales more to their liking. The simple hostels of South Wales are renowned for being "what hostelling is all about", and this had recognition when the group of four hostels in the Elenith (Bryn Poeth, Dolgoch, Tyncornel and Blaencaron) received priority treatment during 1988 and 1989.

Membership of YHA is desirable but not absolutely essential. 1990 fees are - senior £7.60, 16-20 £4, 5-15 £1.70. If only one or two nights are contemplated a guest pass fee can be paid costing just over a third of the membership fee and lasting two nights.

Overnight fees vary according to the scale rate for the hostel. 1990 fees on the Cambrian Way hostels vary from £3.20 at the simple, scale 1, hostels up to £5.60 for scale 7 hostels at Cardiff and Pen-y-pass. 16 to 20 age members pay about 80% of senior rate. Booking in advance is normally direct to the warden but at the time of writing is to the regional office at Cardiff for Tyncornel and Rowen. There are separate booking bureaux for the Brecon Beacon hostels through Llwyn-y-celyn hostel warden, and for the Elenith hostels from Bryn Poeth to Ystumtuen through the regional office. Details are given in the YHA Accommodation Guide on the respective hostel area pages. Telephone bookings cannot be guaranteed without payment, and should only be made during hostel opening hours (before 1000 and after 1700) and preferably not during meal times. Firm bookings by telephone can be made using Access or Visa cards, except at Bryn Poeth Uchaf, Tyncornel, Ystumtuen and Rowen. All hostels can be full in holiday periods but meals-provided hostels can also get booked up in May, June and early July with school parties. Be particularly watchful of weekly closing nights for warden's day off. Some hostels have a self-cooking night and other hostels are open all the week. Very few hostels are open in the winter months, though some, especially smaller hostels, may be willing to open for parties of five or more.

At the hostels where meals are provided, these cannot be guaranteed unless booked and paid for in advance. The evening meal can sometimes be booked if arrival is made before 6 p.m. The evening meal is at a set time, usually 7 p.m. All hostels have a members kitchen where all utensils are provided for preparing, cooking and eating meals. Most hostels have stores of basic food to sell but at the remoter hostels too much reliance should not be placed on them - see notes under individual hostels. Fresh milk and bread should be ordered in advance but are often available on arrival.

Sleeping is in dormitories of varying sizes. Sexes are segregated, but at some hostels there are small rooms which the wardens can allow for family use. All hostellers must use a sheet sleeping bag. These can be hired for 75p at hostels.

Camping is allowed at some hostels at half the senior bednight fee regardless of age. Campers can use the hostel facilities but must not take hostel bedding or utensils to their tents.

Booking into hostels can be up to 10.30p.m. Hostellers are expected to be in by 11 and lights out is usually at 11.30 p.m. Rising before 7.0 a.m. is frowned on. Tell the warden if you want to make an early getaway. Times are generally more flexible at the smaller more remote hostels.

Twenty hostels are listed below. Some are too close together to be used by all except very slow walkers but the average keen hosteller is likely to use about fourteen. Very regrettably four hostels have closed down in recent years and have not been replaced. The first to close was Gerddi Bluog in the Rhinogau. This was partly opened with Cambrian Way in mind but its closure due to lack of support poses the most difficult accommodation problem on the whole route.

Crickhowell was the next to close, when the historic building was suddenly found to be dangerous and too expensive for YHA to repair. The bitterest blow however was Dinas Mawddwy, a large and efficient self-cooking hostel in a superb situation and a key hostel for Cambrian Way. The author backed a loser here by spending many, albeit enjoyable, days trying to improve the hostel only to be defeated by an ultimate liability for YHA to renew the large roof. With hindsight the time might have been better spent writing this guide book at an earlier date instead of waiting for the Countryside Commission to get an agreed route, and then giving up. Harlech closed in 1989. Further hostels may be closed as YHA seeks to retain economic viability and to capitalise on its more valuable properties.

YHA Offices and Shop

Youth Hostels Association (England & Wales) National Office, Trevelyan House, 8 St. Stephens Hill, St. Albans, Herts, AL1 2DY. Tel.St. Albans (0727)55215. For membership & accommodation guide.

Wales Region. Office, 1 Cathedral Rd., Cardiff, CF1 9HA. Tel. Cardiff (0222)396766 for hostel enquiries, bookings for Tyncornel and Rowen, and for Elenith booking bureau.

YHA Adventure Shop, 13 Castle St. (opposite the Castle), Cardiff, Tel.(0222)399178. Open Mon-Sat. 9.30 to 5.30. For enrolments and large selection of walking and camping equipment, including sheet sleeping bags.

Hostels by or near the Cambrian Way (1990 information)

Cardiff at ST184789, 1 Wedal Rd., Roath Park, Cardiff, scale 7. Tel.(0222)462303, 68 beds. This hostel was only opened in 1986 and is already proving very popular with the internationals, so booking can be important. EM 6.30pm plus cafeteria service July/August only. No closing night between March and October. Two miles from start of Cambrian Way covered by buses.

Llwyn-y-pia, Rhondda Valley, at SS993939 (1:50,000 map 170), 62 beds, scale 5. Tel. Tonypandy (0443)430859. Hostel quarter of a mile from station. EM7.0pm (not Sundays). Closing night Sunday, except July and August. Glyncornel Environmental Studies Centre and hostel are in a former mineowner's house, more recently a hospital, in extensive wooded grounds above industrialised valley. Hostel is near the area immortalised in "How Green was my Valley". There is a mining museum at the hostel. Although 14 miles from the Cambrian Way at Tongwynlais, trains run regularly to and from Radyr and Taffs Well.

Capel-y-ffin, Black Mountains, at SO250328, 38 beds plus camping, scale 3. Tel.Crucorney (0873)890650. EM7.30pm. Bread and milk must be ordered at least a week in advance. Closed every Wednesday, except July/August and Easter. Resident warden. Good drying facilities, showers. This homely and magnificently situated hostel is in a former farmhouse converted from King George VI Memorial Fund. It is popular for pony trekking and Offa's Dyke path walkers, so booking is important.

Llwyn-y-celyn (pronounced "thlooinakellin"), Brecon Beacons, at SS973225, 46 beds, scale 3. Tel. Brecon(0874)4261. Resident warden provides snack meals. Closed Sundays except bank holiday weekends. Like Capel-y-ffin, this hostel was once the highest farm in its valley. Attractive surroundings with scattered natural woodland around and nature reserve nearby.

Ystradfellte (pronounced "Ustradvethta"), south of Brecon Beacons at SN925127, 28 beds, simple, scale 1. Tel. Glyn Neath (0639)720301. Closed Thursday except mid-July to end of August. No meals provided. Bread and milk not available (shop/PO near church and pub at 930134). Common room and one dormitory in house across the road. Almost the only accommodation in the very fine waterfall and cave country that is well worth a day's stopover.

Llanddeusant (pronounced "Thlandysant") at SN776245, 26 beds, simple, scale 1. Tel. Gwynfe (05504)634. No closing night. No meals provided. Hot shower. Hostel was once the Old Red Lion Inn, but it is difficult to imagine how this tiny hamlet supported a pub. Nearest shop and telephone 1½ miles away. Stock up at Llwyn-y-celyn or Ystradfellte. No bread or milk.

Bryn Poeth Uchaf, Rhandirmwyn, at SN796439, 26 beds, including a family unit, simple, scale 1. Tel.(warden) Cynghordy (05505)235. No meals provided. No closing night. Book in at warden's farmhouse, Hafod-y-pant (SN800432), then follow waymarked path for three-quarters of a mile up to hostel, which is an old farmhouse, lit by gaslight and very isolated. Views back to Brecon Beacons. Most remote of the hostels as no vehicular access. Warden has no stores and does not sell bread or milk, so stock up in Llandovery. Drying facilities if you light the fire. Hot shower. Waymarked path on to Rhandirmwyn.

Tyncornel, Elenith, at SN751534, 18 beds, simple, scale 1. No telephone. No meals provided. No closing night. Only way of booking in advance is by post to Regional Office. In some respects more remote than Bryn Poeth though there is a long rough road to the hostel. Stock up at the post office at Rhandirmwyn (next shops at Pontrhydfendigaid unless detour is made to Tregaron). Hostel is former farmhouse but common room and members' kitchen are still in separate rooms downstairs unlike Bryn Poeth where ground floor has been made into a kitchen/common room. Gas lighting, drying facilities if you light the fire. Hot shower.

Dolgoch, Elenith, at SN806561, 22 beds, simple, scale 1. Tel. Tregaron (0974)298680. No meals provided. No closing night. Resident warden. Hot shower, small store. Although well off the route this old farmhouse can be rung up to ascertain availability of beds.

Blaencaron at SN713608, 16 beds, simple, scale 1. This hostel was noted as being in a primitive class all on its own. Some hostellers went there because you had to get water from the stream and walk round the back of the old school building to a chemical toilet. A past voluntary steward is said to have taken the water supply out of the hostel because it was getting too civilised. Hostel Standards Committee, however, just cannot abide such eccentricity and demanded the closure of the hostel. The South Wales Region of YHA put up a terrific fight and the Countryside Commission came up with a 50% grant for a complete internal rearrangement, including running water, flush toilets, drying facilities and hot shower. The hostel reopened in spring 1985. No meals or food are provided and there is no closing night. All food must be brought. The warden lives at a farm nearer Tregaron. (Tel.Tregaron(0974)298441.)

Ystumtuen (pronounced "Ustumteean"), at SN735786, 24 beds, simple scale 1. Tel. (warden) Ponterwyd (097085)693. No meals provided. No closing night. This hostel is an old village school with a spacious well-appointed kitchen/common room. Toilets are up the garden path. Drying cupboard with fan heater. The quiet village was once a scene of much lead mining but all that is cleared away now. There is a very

interesting mining museum and a cafe three miles away at Llywernog,
SN733809. The warden lives nearby and has a small store.

Corris at SH753080, 42 beds, simple scale 1. Tel. Corris (065473)
686. No meals provided, small store at hostel and PO/shop in village
(ECD Wed.). Another former school. Closing night Tuesday. A family
room is sometimes available. Showers. Corris is a former slate quarry-
ing village in spectacular wooded surroundings. It has a railway museum
and a craft centre, and 2½ miles to the south is the Centre for Alternative Technology. Divergence from the main route can be made at
Mynydd Ceiswyn, thence via Cwm Ratgoed and Aberllefenni making 11.3
miles from Dinas Mawddwy. Corris to Cader Idris involves a minimum
of 1.2 miles of the A487 and distances are 9.1 miles to Kings (plus
2933' of ascent) and 14 miles to Barmouth.

Kings, Dolgellau, at SH683161, 56 beds, camping, scale 3. Tel.
Dolgellau(0341)422392. Showers. Closing night Sunday except July,
August and bank holiday weekends. EM 7.0p.m. House in idyllic
wooded valley setting with river running through grounds. Some dormitories in large refurbished outbuilding. Check on access into house
and kitchen if leaving early in morning. Members' kitchen can get congested. Strategically awkwardly placed for next night's stop unless
camping on the Rhinogs or diverging to Llanbedr.

Llanbedr at SH585267, 47 beds, family room, scale 3. Tel.
Llanbedr (034123)287. Showers. EM 7.0p.m. Closing night Fri. May/
June, except bank holiday weekends. House by main road where it
crosses river Artro.

Ffestiniog at SH704427, 60 beds, family room, scale 3. Tel.
Ffestiniog (076676)2765. Showers. EM 7.0p.m. Closing night Thursday
July-Sept., Sunday other months except bank holiday weekends.

Bryn Gwynant at SH641513, 70 beds, family room, camping, scale 5.
Tel. Beddgelert (076686)251. Showers. EM 7.0p.m. plus snack service.
Closing night Sunday except Apr.-Sept. Men's dormitories in annex.
Stone built mansion in 40 acres of grounds overlooking Llyn Gwynant.
Good drying facilities.

Pen-y-pass at SH647556, 117 beds, family room, scale 7, limited
daytime access. Tel. Llanberis (0286)870428. Showers. EM 7.0p.m.
Formerly a famous climbers' pub on the pass, converted and added to
at great expense to become the largest hostel in Snowdonia. At least
the pass is quieter in the evening after the hordes who walk up
Snowdon from here have gone away.

Idwal Cottage, Ogwen, at SH648603, 56 beds, family room, scale 4.
Tel. Bethesda (0248)600225. Showers. EM 7.0p.m. Closing night
Sunday except July/August and bank holiday weekends. Not exactly a
cottage. Some dormitories in old chapel nearby. Mountain rescue post.
Spectacular situation at focal point of wild and popular mountain area.

Ro Wen (also spelt "Roewen"), North Carneddau, at SH747721, 27
beds, simple, scale 1. Tel.Conwy (0492)531406. No meals provided.
Open May-August closing night Tuesday. Hurray for return to a small
hostel. A gem set half way up side of Tal-y-fan, in an old farmhouse.
Enables the long trek across the Carneddau to be broken up leaving a
half day on to the finish at Conwy. No stores, bread or milk. Shop is
1½ miles on and 700' below. Advance booking through regional office.

Penmaenmawr, North Wales coast, at SH737780, 56 beds, family room,
camping, scale 3. Tel.Penmaenmawr (0492)623476. EM 7.0p.m. Closing
night Sunday May/June, Wednesday July-Sept. Cool your feet off in
the sea. Wooden building in extensive grounds, once a holiday home
for workers from Pilkington glassworks.

ACCOMMODATION AND SERVICES

Including:
    Bed and breakfast addresses, small hotels
    Inns providing meals, cafes, fish and chips shops
    Camp sites
    Shops in villages and post offices
    A taxi service
    Youth hostels (listed without detail, see pages 82-85)

No fee has been accepted for any entry, and the list is provided
purely as a service to Cambrian Way walkers. Entry is at the entire
discretion of the author, who nevertheless accepts no responsibility for
accuracy of the entries or the standard of service provided. Most of
the establishments have been personally visited, and will be visited
again from time to time. Prices with the year in which they were obtained, are only intended as a guide and will certainly be more by the
time the guide is used.

Amendments may be included with late information on the inside
back cover.

Comments on all services used, both good and bad, are particularly
welcome to the author (address page 95).

Place names are given in capitals, followed by the postal address
and county, e.g. LLANTHONY, Abergavenny, Gwent.

Grid references follow the name of the establishment, e.g. SO277141,
the explanation of which is in the key to the Ordnance Survey
Landranger series (1:50,000) maps.

Telephone Number (T) - exchange is the place name unless otherwise stated.

Rooms - the number available is given. S=single room, D=room
with double bed, T=room with two beds, F=room with accommodation
for three or more people, usually 1 double bed and 1 single bed.

ES - room with private toilet, and bath and/or shower.

TMF =tea making facilities available.

Meals - EM=evening meal available, O=if ordered in advance.
SB=snacks at bar. PL=packed lunch available.

Early closing day (ECD) - most village shops have an early closing
day. These are given when known. In towns there are usually
food shops open even on an early closing day.

CARDIFF, South Glamorgan
    Accommodation list from City Hall, Cardiff.
    Youth Hostel, ST184789. 68 beds - see separate list.
    24 Pasturton Gardens, (off Cathedral Rd.) ST170769, Mrs. Jones,
       T.395342. £10(89) S2 T1. Breakfast fm. 0730.
    39 Pasturton Gardens, ST170769, Mrs.George, T.383660. £9(88)
       T2 D1 F2 TMF EMO. Breakfast fm. 0730.
    Coniston, 11 Dyfig St., ST171772, Mrs. Heron, T.232249, £9(88)
       S2 T1 D1 TMF. Breakfast 8-9.
    Numerous other houses in Cathedral Rd. area.
    Peppermill Restaurant ST167770 EM except Sunday.

TONGWYNLAIS, Cardiff
Three pubs and fish and chip shop. ST133822.

LLWYNYPIA, Rhondda Valley, Mid.Glam. (By train from Radyr
or Taffs Well)
Youth Hostel, Glyncornel Centre, SS993939, see separate list.

THORNHILL, Caerphilly, Mid-Glamorgan
Travellers Rest. ST158843. T.(0222)886894. SB, no accommodation.

RUDRY, Caerphilly, Mid-Glamorgan
Maenllwyd Inn, ST201866, SB. No accommodation.
Griffin Motel ST193866. T.Caerphilly 883396. £32S £45D(£40 at WE)
(89) Restaurant.

MACHEN, Newport, Gwent
Brynteg, White Hart, ST204891. Mr.T.E.Jones, T.(0633)440280.
£11(88), S1 D2 T1. EM 3mins. walk.

NEWPORT, Gwent (bus stop for Risca Oakfield Rd. ST302879)
Abbotsfield Guest House, 13 Bryngwyn Rd. ST304880, Mrs. Walters,
T.(0633)259311. D1 T2 Fr.£9.50(89).
Caerleon House Hotel, Caerau Rd. ST304878. Mrs. Powell,
T.(0633)264869. D£13 S£17. Showers, TV, TMF.
Tainlord Guest House, 41 Caerau Rd. ST304877. Mrs. Miguel
T.(0633)262831. £9.50(89) S2 D1 T1.
Arundel, 26 Chepstow Rd. ST318885. Mrs.Harrington,
T.(0633)267297. S4 D3 £11S £10D(89).

RISCA, Newport, Gwent
Westwood Villa Guest House, 59 Risca Rd., Crosskeys, NP1 7BT.
ST223917. Bob & Maureen Evans, T.(0495)270336. S1 F4
Fm£12(90) TMF.

Cwmcarn Hotel, Pontywaun, ST220929, Mr.Sheehan, T.(0495)270418.
Darren Inn, ST234915. SB. No accommodation.
Italian take-away ST238905.
Nant Carn Valley Camp Site (Islwyn Borough Council) ST230935.
Toilets, wash basins, £1.70 per tent (88).

PONTYPOOL, Gwent (ECD M/Th)
Mountain Air Inn, ST277979. No meals or accommodation.
Cafe at Sports Centre ST286007.

MAMHILAD, Pontypool, Gwent
Ty'r Ywen Fach Farm, GR296046. Mrs. Armitage, T.Little Mill
(049528)200. D1 F1 £15 ES. EM£6 (89).

LITTLE MILL, Pontypool, Gwent
Pentwyn Farm, SO325035. T.Little Mill(049528)249. D1 T1 F1
Fm.£11.50. EMO £7. (90)

ABERGAVENNY, Gwent
Halidon House, Monmouth Rd. SO303137. Mrs.Heritage T.77855.
S1 D2 T1 F1. TMF Swimming pool (May-Sept.) £15(89).
Brookfield, 16 Monmouth Rd., NP7 5HH. SO303137 Mrs.Randall,
T.(0873)77972. S1 T2 £11.50(88).
Bryn Usk, 28 Monmouth Rd., NP7 5HL. SO304136 Mrs. Bowdler,
T.(0873)2739. S1 D1 F1 EMO.
Thornbury Hotel, Brecon Rd., SO294146. Mrs.Hemming T.(0873)
2608. D4 F3 £13.50(88). SB EM Small parties.
Pyscodlyn Farm SO266156. Camping.

LLANTHONY, Abergavenny, Gwent
Half Moon Inn, SO286279. T.Abergavenny (0873)890611. D4 T3
£15(89) EM SB.
Abbey Hotel, NP7 7NP, SO288278. T.Abergavenny (0873)890487.
£15(89).
Court Farm, SO288277. Camping.
Maes-y-beran Farm, SO299266. Mr.Morgan, T.Abergavenny
(0873)890283. D1 F1 S2 £10(89) EMO.

CAPEL-Y-FFIN, Abergavenny, Gwent
Youth Hostel, 38 beds, see separate list.
Grange Pony Trekking Centre, SO251315. Mrs.Griffiths, T.Aberga-
venny (0873)890215. T2 F3 £13(90) EM£4.
Chapel Farm, SO254315. Camping.

PENGENFORDD, Talgarth, Powys
Cwmfforest Guest Farm (Riding centre) SO182292, Mrs.Turner,
T.Talgarth 711398. 2 or 3 rooms usually available, check by
'phone. EM.
The Castle Inn, SO174296. Doug.&Beryl Webb. Talgarth (0874)
711353. Camping SB. No accommodation.

CWMDU, Crickhowell, Powys
Dol Fawr Farm, SO183266. Mrs. Powell, T.Bwlch(0874)730684.
£7.50(88). T1 D1 F1 EMO. Easter-Oct.

TRETOWER, Crickhowell, Powys
Tretower Court Inn, SO185215. T.Bwlch(0874)730204. S1 D2 T1
£14S £25D(89) EM.

CRICKHOWELL, Powys
Dragon Hotel, SO217183. T.(0873)810362. S2 D7 T2 Fr.£11.50(88) EM.
Glan-Nant, Brecon Rd., SO214191. Mrs.Usborne, T.810631. S1 T2
Apr.-Oct. Price on application.
10 Llangenny Lane, SO222182. Mrs.Mundy, T.(0873)810183. S1 D2
£8.50(88).
Riverside Caravan & Camping Park, New Rd., NP8 1AY, SO215184.
Mar.1st-Oct.31st. Fr.£2.50 per tent(88). Caravan per night
if not let.

LLANGATTOCK, Crickhowell, Powys
Ty Croeso Guest House, Dardy, NP8 1PU, SO206183. T.Crick-
howell (0873)810573. S2 D3 T3 F1 £14(88). Parties catered for.

CWM CRAWNON
Pyrgad SO101159. Mr.Probert, T.Brecon(0874)730558. Camping.
Water, no facilities.

TORPANTAU, Merthyr Tydfil, Mid. Glam.
Ty Neuadd, Neuadd Reservoirs, SN030186. Mr.P.W.Whittaker,
T.Merthyr Tydfil (0685)71889. S1 D1 T1 £12(89) EMO PL.

LIBANUS, Brecon, Powys
Youth Hostel, Llwyn-y-celyn. 46 beds. See separate list.

YSTRADFELLTE, Aberdare, Mid-Glam.
Youth Hostel, Tal'r Heol. 28 beds - see separate list.
Post Office, SN930134. T.Glyn Neath(0639)720269. ECD Sat.
Teas, light meals.
Maesyronnen, CF44 9JE, SN929135. Mrs. Morgan, T.Glyn Neath
(0639)722343. S1 D1 £9(89).

GLYNTAWE, Aber-craf, Swansea, West Glam.
  Dan-yr-ogof Caves Motel, SA9 1GJ, SN840161. Apr.-Oct. only.
    T.Abercrave (0639)730284. Room and breakfast (9.0 a.m.)
    £10(88) TMF EMO.
  Dan-yr-ogof camping ground, SN843163 Apr.-Oct.
  Gwyn Arms, SN846165. T.Abercrave (0639)730310. Camping,toilets,
    water. SB (not Su., check other days in advance)
  Tafarn-y-garreg Inn, SN849171. T.Abercrave (0639)730267, SB
    summer only. Check as above.

CRAI, Brecon, Powys
  Llwynhir Farm, LD3 8YW, SN893242. Mrs. Harris, T.Sennybridge
    (087482)563. D2 £11(89) EMO.

LLANDDEUSANT, Llangadog, Dyfed
  Youth Hostel, Old Red Lion, 28 beds - see separate list.
  Blaenau Farm, SN794241. Mrs. Dobbs, T.Gwynfe (05504)277.
    3-berth caravans. £6.90 per night.
  Cross Inn, SN773258. T.Gwynfe (05504)621, Camping, caravans, shop.

MYDDFAI, Llandovery, Dyfed.
  Plough Inn, SA20 0NZ, SN772301. T.Llandovery (0550)20643.
    S2 D2 £9.50(89) EMO SB.
  Gollen-wen Farm, SA20, SN766308. Mrs.Powell, T.Llandovery
    (0550)20162. S1 D1 T1 F1 £10(89) EMO Mar.-Oct.

LLANDOVERY, Dyfed.
  Royston Hotel, High St., SN769343. T.(0550)20435. S1 D2 F2
    £10(89) EMO.
  Llwyncelyn Guest House, Chain Bridge, SA20 0EP. SN761347.
    T.(0550)20566. S1 D2 T2 F1 £14(89) EMO.
  Ash Grove, Llangadog Rd. SN761336. Teresa Hay, T.(0550)20136.
    D1 T1 F1 £10(89) PL
  Erwlon Caravan Park, Brecon Rd., SN779343. T.(0550)20332.
    Camping, possibility of caravan for one night, all facilities
    including showers. Open all year.
  Prestbury Lodge, SA20 0JT, SN775340. Sheila & Keith Robinson.
    T.(0550)21009. S1 D2 T1 £12(89) TMF EMO.

RHANDIRMWYN, Llandovery, Dyfed
  Youth Hostel, Bryn Poeth Uchaf, SN796439, 26 beds - see separate list.
  Mia'r Nant, SN786436. Mrs. Price, T.(05506)219. D2 T1 F1 £10(89).
  Royal Oak, SN785437, T.(05506)201. S1 D1 F2 £11.75(89) EM SB.
  1 Nantymwyn Terrace, SN781437. Mrs.Jones, T.(05506)202. 4-berth
    caravan. Terms by arrangement.
  Bryn Hyfryd, SN773438, Mrs.Whiskerd, no 'phone but can be
    contacted on (05506)215. 3-berth caravan, terms by arrangement.
  Post Office Stores, SN785437. Open 8.0-8.0(6.30 in winter). Milk,
    bread, all groceries, fruit.
  Caravan/campsite, SN779436, T,(05506)257.
  Nantybai Mill, SN774445. Anthea Jones, T.(05506)211. D1 £7.50(87)
    teas.
  Broncwrt, SN768448 (note not house marked Bron-y-cwrt on
    OS 1:50,000) Mr.Davis T.(05506)227. Camping £1 per tent.

DOETHIE & UPPER TWYI VALLEYS
  Tyncornel Youth Hostel, SN751534. 18 beds - see separate list.
  Dolgoch Youth Hostel, SN806561. 20 beds - see separate list.

TREGARON, Dyfed
  Blaencaron Youth Hostel, SN713608. 18 beds - see separate list.
  Cambrian Coffee Shop, Chapel St., SY25 6HD. Mrs.Knight,
    T.(0974) 298637. F1 £9.50(89) EMO £5.50
  Brynawal, Station Rd., SN679599. T.(0974)298310. S1 D1 T1 F2
    £10(89) EM £5.

STRATA FLORIDA, Ystrad Meurig, Dyfed
  Pantywedwyn, SN755650. Mrs.Davis, T.Pontrhydfendigaid
    (09745)358. D1 T1 F1 £18 incl. EM.

PONTRHYDFENDIGAID, Ystrad Meurig, Dyfed
  Heddle Tea Rooms, SN730664. Mrs.Harris T.(09745)686. £9(90)
    S1 T1 F1 EM snacks teas.
  Llys Teg Guest House, SN731668. Mr.&Mrs. Edwards, T.(09745)697.
    S3 D2 T1 F1 £13.50(90) ES EM £7 PL. Small parties catered for.
  Bronceiro, SN732663. T.(09745)230. Camping, showers.

CWMYSTWYTH, Aberystwyth, Dyfed
  Post Office, SN790738. T.Pontrhydigroes (097 422) 231. Open in
    summer until 6.0 p.m. Enquire re camping and B&B.
  Hafod Lodge, SN784742. Colin & Jenny Beard, T.Pontrhydigroes
    (097 422)247. T1 D2 £10(88) EMO £8.
  Gate Cottage, SY23 4AD, SN784742. Eric & Lesley Heyes,
    T.(097 422)227. T1 D1 £10(88) EMO.
  Tainewyddion Uchaf, SN791750. Peg & Red Liford, T.(097 422)672.
    S1 T3 £8(88) EM PL.
  Tyllwyd, SN823753. Mrs.Raw, T.(097 422)216. Camping £1.50 showers.
  Gelmast, SN777756, Mr.Postings, T.(097 422)239. Camping.

DEVIL'S BRIDGE, Aberystwyth, Dyfed
  Mount Pleasant, SN736769. Mr.&Mrs.Sherlock, T.Ponterwyd
    (097 085)219. S1 T2 D2 Fm.£10.50(89) TMF EMO.
  Woodlands Hotel, SY23 3JW, SN745771. T.(097 085)376. S1 D4 F3 T1
    £10(88) EM BS. Take away meals, b'fasts for campers.
  Woodlands Camp Site, SN746774.
  Post Office/shop, SN738769. T.(097 085)228. 9-5.30 ECD Sat. also
    Wed. in winter. Open Sun. 2-6p.m. in summer. Teas, snacks.
  Llysamaeth, SN736770. Mrs.Davies, T.(097 085)297. F1 £11(90).
    Poss. flat sleeping four.
  Penlonfedw, SN736763. T.(097 085)241. Camping, toilet, water.
    Butcher, grocer, sells camping Gaz.
  Porthilenydd, SN743767. T.(097 085)239. Beds for nine
    Fr.£9.50(88) EM £5.50.

YSTUMTUEN, Aberystwyth, Dyfed
  Youth Hostel, SN735786. 24 beds - see separate list.

PONTERWYD, Aberystwyth, Dyfed
  Dyffryn Castell Hotel, SN775817. T.Ponterwyd (097 085)237.
    Seven rooms, £14.50-£16.50(89).
  PO/shop, SN750808. 9-5.30. ECD Wed. & Sat.

DYLIFE, Llanbrynmair, Powys
  Star Inn, SN863940. T.Llanbrynmair (06503)345, Tony Banks.
    S2 D3 T2 Fr.£12(90) SB.
  Maesmedrisiol Farm, Staylittle, SN884945. Mrs.B.Anwyl,
    T.Llanbrynmair (06503)270. S1 D1 F1 £10(90) EMO.

LLANBRYNMAIR, Powys
  Dolgadfan, SN883002. Mrs.Anwyl, T.Llanbrynmair (06503)245
    S2 D2 T1 F1 £12(90) EMO. Camping.
  Cyfeiliog Guest House, Bont Dolgadfan, SY19 7BB, SN886003. Liz &
    Andrew Fox, T.(06503)231 T2 F1 £10.50(90) EMO£6.50.
    Transport arranged to and from Cambrian Way.

COMMINS COCH, Machynlleth, Powys
  Post Office/stores SH844032.
  Gwalia, Cemmaes, SH853048. Mrs. Chandler, T. Cemmaes Road
    (06502)377. T1 F1 £10(90) EM£6. Vegetarian, limited camping.

CEMMAES, Machynlleth, Powys
  Bron-y-gan, SH836057. Mrs.Lloyd-Lewis, T.Cemmaes Rd.(06502)237.
    D2 F1 £9(88). 6-berth caravan £8 per night.

MALLWYD, Machynlleth, Powys
  Brigands Inn, SH863125. T.Dinas Mawddwy (06504)208. S3 D10 F2
    £16.95(90) some ES, SB.
  PO/shop. Small super-market at garage.
  Gwernhefn, SH856112. Mrs.R.Morgans, T.Cemmaes Rd. (06502)465.
    6-berth caravan £8.50 per night.
  Ty-mawr, SH855107. Mrs.M.Morgans, T.(06502)419. 6-berth caravan,
    £8.50 per night.

DINAS MAWDDWY, Machynlleth, Powys
  Celyn Brithion Caravan Site, SH861139. Mrs.Rees, T.Dinas Mawddwy
    (06504)344. Camping.
  Buckley Arms Hotel, SH859140. T.(06504)261. S1 D6 T2 Fr.£18(90) SB.
  Shop at garage opposite hotel open daily late in evening.
  Tawelfan, SH858147, Mrs. Marshall, T.(06504)371. D2 T1 £7.50(87).
  Red Lion, SH859148. T.(06504)247/260. D2 T2 F1 £9.50(87) EM SB.
  Tremynfa, SH858147. Mrs.Rees, T.(06504)240. D2 T1 £7.50(87).
  PO/shop ECD Thúrs.

(CROSS FOXES), Dolgellau, Gwynedd
  Cross Foxes Inn, Brithdir, SH766167. T.Dolgellau (0341)422487.
    D2 T1 F1 £11.50(90) EM SB camping.

DOLGELLAU, Gwynedd
  Penbryn Croft, Cader Rd., SH725177. Mrs.A.Jones, T.Dolgellau
    (0341)422815. D2 T3 F1 £10(88) EMO
  Dwy Olwyn, Coed y Fronallt, LL4 2YG. SH734183. Mrs.N.Jones,
    T.(0341) 422822. T2 D1 F1 Fr.£8.50(88) EMO PL
  Tan-y-fron Caravan & Camping Park, Arran Rd., SH735176.
    T.(0341)422638. Camping, also B.&B. D1 T1 F1 £8.50(88).

CORRIS, Machynlleth, Powys
  Youth Hostel. SH753080. 42 beds - see separate list.
  London House, SH756078. Mrs.Reynolds, T.(065 473)625 D2 T1 £8.50(90)
  Braich Goch Hotel, SH753075. T.(065 473)229. S1 D3 T2 Fm.£15(90)
    EM SB.
  Rhianfa Guest House, Corris Uchaf, SH744088. Mrs. Sweeney, T.
    (065 473)283. S1 D1 T1 F2 £9.50(89) EM£5 PL. Terms for parties.
  Ty-r Graig, SH754077. Mrs.Stieler, T.(065 473)669. S1 D1.

TAL-Y-LLYN, Twywn, Gwynedd
  Cwm-rhwyddfor Farm, Minfordd, SH737120. Mrs.Nutting, T.Corris
    (065 473) 286/380. Camping. Also B&B.
  Dol Einion, SH729113. Marian Rees. T.Corris 312. Camping, shower.
  Dolffanog Fach, SH729105. Mrs.Pughe, T.Corris 235. D1 F2 S1 £9(87) EM.
  Dolffanog Fawr Guest House, SH729105. T.Corris 247, Mrs.Ashby.
    D2 T1 £10.50(87) EMO TMF.

Dolffanog Fach, SH729105. Mrs.Pughe, T.Corris 235. D1 F2 S1 £9(87) EM.
Dolffanog Fawr Guest House, SH729105. T.Corris 247. Mrs.Ashby.
D2 T1 £10.50(87) EMO TMF.

ISLAWEDREF, Dolgellau, Gwynedd
Gilfachwydd, SH709161. Mrs. Eastland, T.Dolgellau (0341)422664.
Camping.
Gwernan Lake Hotel, SH704159. T.Dolgellau (0341)422488. S5 D6
Fr.£15(89). Minimum two nights at Bank Holidays. EM.
Ty'n-y-ceunant, SH689152. Mrs.Rees, T.(0341)422300. Self-catering
unit for four £12p.n.(own sleeping bags). 4-berth caravan £4,
camping. (89).
Tyddynmawr, SH703154. Mrs.Evans, T.(0341)422331. D2 £10(87).
Kings Youth Hostel, SH683160. 56 beds - see separate list.

ARTHOG, Dolgellau, Gwynedd
Pen-y-rodyn, SH637141. Mrs. Bradbury, T.Fairbourne (0341)250659.
D2 T1 F1 Fr.£14.50(89) EM £8.25(89).
Garthyfog Camping Site, SH636139. £2.25 per tent. Small caravan.

BARMOUTH, Gwynedd
Bay View, 6 Porkington Terrace, LL42 1LY, SH619156. Colin &
Vera Portman, T.(0341)280284. D1 T2 F1 Fm.£8(89) EMO.
Tal-y-carreg, 8 Porkington Terrace, LL42 1EN, SH619156. John &
Norma Stockford, T.(0341)280742. D2 T1 £9.50(89).
Several others on front, Marine Parade, SH610159.

CWM NANTCOL, Llanbedr, Gwynedd
Craig Isaf, SH635259. Mr.Jones, T.Llanbedr (034123)341. Camping.

LLANBEDR, Gwynedd
Youth Hostel, 47 beds. SH585267 - see separate list.
Yr Hen Feudy Cottage, LL45 2LI. T.(0341)23596. T1 F2 £10(88).
The Mill, SH589268. Mrs. Roberts. Camping, caravans to let.

HARLECH, Gwynedd
Castle Cottage, SH582313. T.(0766)780479. D2 F2 £17ES(90) EM.
Tyddyn Gwynt, Mrs. Jones, T.(0766)780296. S1 D1 T1 F1 EM.
Taxi service Cwm Bychan or Cwm Nantcol approx. £6 ea. way (88).
M.G.Parry, Tan-y-allt (opp. station) T.(0766)780392.

CWM BYCHAN, LLanbedr, Gwynedd
Camping SH646314. No facilities.

TRAWSFYNYDD, Gwynedd
White Lion, SH707357. M.Kreft, T.(0766)87277. T1 F3 £10(88) SB.
Clifton House, SH707358. Mrs. Jones, T.(0766)87261, T2 S1 £9(88)EMO.
Trawsfynydd Holiday Village, SH716319. T.(0766)87219. Log cabins.
Drying room. Pub. at top of holiday village meals and take away.

Gellilydan, Blaenau Ffestiniog, Gwynedd
Bryntirion, SH680391. Mrs.Evans, T.(0766)85321. Apply for terms.
S1 D1 T1 EMO.
Llwyn Farm, SH683392. Camping.
Gwyfryn, SH684398. Mrs.G.Jones, T.(0766)87225. S1 D1 F1
£9.50(89) EMO TMF.
Bryn Arms, SH685396. Bar meals.

MAENTWROG, Blaenau Ffestiniog, Gwynedd
Post Office, Bron-y-wern, SH665405. Mrs.Jackson, T.(0766)85210.
D1 T1 S2 £8.50(89).
Old Rectory Hotel, SH665407. T.(0766)85305. D8 Fr.£15(89) EM.

Oakley Arms, SH661409. T.(0766)85277. D3 T2 F4 Fm.£12.50(89)
EM SB to 9.15 p.m.
The White Barn, Tan Y Bwlch, SH659408. Richard Ratcliffe, T.Maen-
twrog (076685)391. D1 F1 £15.50(89) EM SB TMF. Lunches, teas.
Llechrwd, SH678413. Mrs.Edwards. Camping £1.50 each. Shower.
Plas Tan Y Bwlch, Snowdonia National Park Study Centre, SH655406.
T.Maentwrog (076685)324. £13(89). Check in advance for accommodation.

FFESTINIOG, Blaenau Ffestiniog, Gwynedd
Pengwrn Arms Hotel, LL41 4PB, SH702420. Ian & Winos Sanderson,
T.(076676)2722. S3 D3 T2 F1 Fr.£12(89) EM.
Newborough House Hotel, Church Square, SH700419. T.(076676)2682.
D2 T3 £10(89) EMO£5.
Youth Hostel, 60 beds. SH704427 - see separate list.

BEDDGELERT, Gwynedd
Plas Colwyn, LL55 4UY, SH589482. T.(076686)458, Mrs.Osmond,
S1 D2 T1 F2 Fr.£10(89) EM £6.
Plas Tan-y-craig, SH591482. B.&G.Maddison, T.(076686)329.
F6 Fr.£10(89) EM£5.50 PL£2.
Colwyn, SH589482. Mrs.Williams, T.(076686)276. S2 D2 T1 F1
Fr.£11(89) EMO.
Craflwyn Hall, SH601491. Mrs.Nemrow, T.(076686)221. Camping.

NANT GWYNANT, Caernarfon, Gwynedd
Bryn Dinas, LL55 4NH, SH625503. Jerry & Barbara Rogers,
T.(076686)234. Bunk beds for 23 in house £4.95ea.(89), for 26
in timber cabins £3.95ea.(89). Own sleeping bag & pillow case
essential. Kitchen in house, also in separate bunkhouse. Meals
can be provided. Booking essential.
Glan Gwynant Country Guest House, SH639514. T.(076686)440.
D2 T2 F1 £10(89) EM£5.50 PL.
Youth Hostel - 70 beds, SH641513 - see separate list.

PEN-Y-PASS
Youth Hostel - 117 beds, SH647556 - see separate list.

OGWEN, Gwynedd
Idwal Cottage Youth Hostel, 56 beds, SH648603 - see separate list.
Gwern Gof Uchaf, SH673603. Camping.
Gwern Gof Isaf, SH685601. Camping.

ROEWEN, Conwy, Gwynedd
Youth Hostel, 27 beds, SH747721 - see separate list.
Compton House, SH758720, Mrs.McQuarrie, T.Tyn-y-groes 650282.
T1 F1 £10(90) EMO£4 PL.

(DWYGYFYCHI), PENMAENMAWR, Gwynedd
Glyn Uchaf, Conwy Old Rd.,SH741765, Mrs.Baxter, T.(0492)623737.
D1 F2 £9.50(87) also chalet, EMO£5.50. Camping if booked.
Penmaenmawr Youth Hostel, SH737780. 56 beds - see separate list.

CONWY, Gwynedd
15 Cadnant Park, SH776777. T.(0492)592319. D3 F3 £10(89).
(Also 13, 25 Cadnant Park, & Llys Gwilym, 3 Mountain Rd., off
Cadnant Park).
Bryn Corach, HF Holidays Ltd., Sychnant Pass Rd., SH775774,
84 beds.

GLOSSARY OF WELSH WORDS AND PLACE NAMES
ON THE CAMBRIAN WAY

aber rivermouth
adar bird
afon river
Agen Allwedd keyhole cave
allt wooded hill
bach small
Beddgelert grave of Gelert (dog)
blaen valley head
bryn hill
Bugeilyn sheep pasture
bwlch mountain pass
Cadair Idris Idris's chair
caer hill fort
Capel-y-ffin chapel on the border
caseg mare
castell castle
carn cairn, heap of stones
Carneddau cairns
Cemais bend in river
Cnewr meandering stream
Cnicht knight
coch red
coed a wood
Commins Coch red commons
craig crag, cliff
crocben gallows
dau & dwy two
ddu & du black
Dduallt black hillside
Dial Garreg stone of revenge
diffwys wilderness, precipice
dinas hill, fortress
Dolgellau meadow of the monks' cells
domen & tomen mound
Drum ridge
drws narrow pass
Dwyryd two fords or streams
Dwygyfylchi two round forts
Dyffryn Castell valley of river Castell
Dylife floods
eglwys church
esgair ridge
faen stone
fan peak
fach small
fawr & mawr large
ffordd road
foel & moel bare hill
Gabalfa ferry
gallt slope
garn cairn
Garn Gron round cairn
gelli grove
glan river
glas blue/green
hafod summer dwelling
Harlech beautiful rock
hendre winter dwelling
is below
isaf lower
Libanus Lebanon
llan church
Llandeusant church of two saints
llethr slope

lluest hill farm, hut
Lluest Ty Mawr hill farm of big house
Llwyn-y-celyn holly grove
Llwyn Onn ash grove
llyn lake
Llywernog place of foxes
maes meadow
Maesteg fair meadow
maen stone
Maentwrog stone of Twrog
Mallwyd grey field
Minffordd edge of road
moel, moelfre bare hill
Myddfai meadow of the round hollow
mynydd mountain
nant brook
newydd new
neuadd mansion
oer cold
ogof cave
oleu light
pant hollow, valley
Pantyfedwen hollow of birch trees
pen peak or top
Penmaenmawr head of the large rock
Pennant head of stream or valley
Pengenffordd head of ridge road
Pen y fan top of the peak
Penygwryd gwryd = length of outstretched arm
plas mansion
Plynlimon (Pumlumon) five peaks
poeth hot
pont & bont bridge
Ponterwyd bridge of poles
Pontarfrynach bridge over river Mynach (monk) (Devil's Bridge)
Pontrhydfendigaid bridge of the blessed one
Pontsticill bridge of the stile
pwll pit, pool
Pysgotwr fishermen
Rhandirmwyn land of minerals
rhiw hillside
rhos moorland
rhyd ford
Ro Wen white pebbles
sarn paved way
scwd waterfall
Sychnant stream that dries up
tal end
Talwrn rocky place, cock fighting pit
Talyllyn end of the lake
Torpantau break in the hollows
Trawsfynydd across the mountain
Tryfan high pointed mountain
Twymyn feverish
ty house
Tyncornel house in a corner
waun moorland, meadow
Waun Oer cold moorland
wen white
ystrad wide valley bottom
Ystradfellte valley of Mellte (swift)
Ysgyfarnogod bare hill of the hares
Yr Wyddfa (Snowdon summit) grave

THE CHECK POINTS

To have walked the Cambrian Way route described in this guidebook it is not necessary to follow the exact route prescribed, in fact individuality is to be encouraged, provided it does not involve trespass. However, to give some yardstick of achievement the following check points must have been visited on a continuous walk, though the walk need not necessarily have been on consecutive days.

1	ST	180765	Cardiff Castle	22	SH	833136	Bwlch Siglen
2	ST	131827	Castell Coch	23	SH	711130	Cader Idris
3	ST	224900	Mynydd Machen	24	SH	620155	Barmouth Bridge
4	ST	242926	Twmbarlwm	25	SH	661258	Y Llethr
5	SO	270119	Blorenge	26	SH	665270	Rhinog Fach
6	SO	272188	Sugar Loaf	27	SH	657290	Rhinog Fawr
7	SO	255315	Capel-y-ffin	28	SH	659347	Moel Ysgyfarnogod
8	SO	225351	Tumpa	29	SH	683359	Moelfryn
9	SO	216290	Waun Fach	30	SH	658449	Moelwyn Mawr
10	SO	207243	Pen Allt Mawr	31	SH	648467	Cnicht
11	SO	192157	Eglwys Faen	32A	SH	594462	Pont Aberglaslyn or
12	SO	012216	Pen y Fan	B	SH	641513	Bryn Gwynant Y.H.
13A	SN	881191	Fan Gihirych or	33	SH	610544	Snowdon
B	SN	408144	Blaen Nedd Isaf junc.	34	SH	643579	Glyder Fawr
14	SN	825218	Bannau Brycheiniog	35	SH	656583	Glyder Fach
15	SN	767447	Towy Bridge	36	SH	666608	Tal-y-llyn - Ogwen
16	SN	740610	Garn Gron	37	SH	663631	Carnedd Dafydd
17	SN	809720	Domen Milwyn	38	SH	684645	Carnedd Llewelyn
18	SN	727782	Pontbren Plwca	39	SH	729727	Tal y Fan
19	SN	790869	Plynlimon	40	SH	760778	Conwy Mountain
20	SN	861940	Dylife	41	SH	783775	Conwy Castle
21	SH	859149	Dinas Mawddwy				

USEFUL ADDRESSES

Ramblers Association. Head Office, 1/5 Wandsworth Rd., London SW8 2XX, 071 582 6878. For membership details and postal sales of this book.
Welsh Officer Pantwood, Pant Lane, Marford, Wrexham, Clwyd LL12 8SG, 0978 855148.

Offa's Dyke Association. Old Primary School, West St., Knighton, Powys, LD7 1EN, 0547 528753. Send s.a.e. for information on Offa's Dyke Path, Glyndwr's Way, map bags (see p.81) and postal sales of this book.

Snowdonia National Park Society. Ty Hyll (Ugly House), Capel Curig, Betws-y-coed, Gwynedd, LL24 0DS, Capel Curig (06904) 287.

National Park Offices. Snowdonia Penrhyndeudraeth, Gwynedd, LL48 6LS, 0766 770274. Brecon Beacons 7 Glamorgan St., Brecon, LD3 7DP, 0874 4437.

Council for the Protection of Rural Wales Ty Gwyn, 31 High St., Welshpool, SY21 7JP, 0938 552525.

Open Spaces Society, 25A Bell St., Henley-on-Thames, Oxon., RG2 2BA, 0491 573535.

County Councils - for path obstruction or maintenance problems:
Gwynedd, Caernarfon, County Surveyor, 0286 4121.
Powys, Llandrindod Wells, Planning Dept., LD1 5ES, 0597 826000.
Dyfed, Llanstephan Road, Carmarthen, 0267 233333.
Gwent, County Hall, Cwmbran, NP44 2XF, Planning Dept. 0633 838838.

The Author A.J.(Tony) Drake, 2 Beech Lodge, Woodleigh, 67 The Park, Cheltenham, Glos., GL50 2RX, 0242 232131.

ABBREVIATIONS

B.&B.	Bed and breakfast	NT	National Trust
Bdy	Boundary	O.S.	Ordnance Survey
BG	Bridle gate	Otw	Old tramway
Br	Bracken	P	Car park
Bn	Barn	p	Limited roadside parking
B.T.C.V.	British Trust for Conservation Volunteers	pa	Path
		PC	Public convenience, toilets
Ca	Cairn		
Cas	Castle	PH	Public house, inn, pub
ECD	Early closing day	PO	Post office and shop
En	Enclosed	R.A.	Ramblers Association
ES	Private toilet &bath &/or shower	Qu	Quarry
		Rd	Tarred road
F	Fence	Res	Reservoir
FB	Footbridge	Rp	Road used as public path
F&C	Fish and chips	R.S.P.B.	Royal Society for the Protection of Birds
FC	Forestry Commission		
FG	Field gate	Ru	Ruined building
Fm	Farm	Sh	Shop
FmRd	Farm road	Sn	Stone
FoRd	Forest road	SP	Signpost
G	Gate	St	Stile
GL	Green lane	Sta	Railway station
HG	Hunting gate (about 3' wide)	Tr	Track
i	Information bureau	T	Telephone callbox
ind	Indistinct	Und	Undefined route
int	Intermittent	UTd	Untarred road
KG	Kissing gate	Wm.	Waymarked path
LS	Ladder stile	Y.H.A.	Youth Hostels Association
MeF	Mesh fence (pig netting)		

KEY TO STRIP MAPS

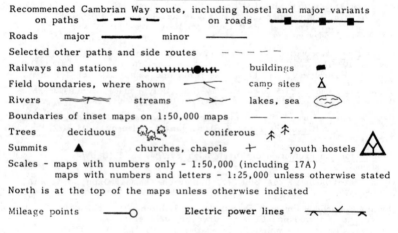

Recommended Cambrian Way route, including hostel and major variants
on paths ▬ ▬ ▬ ▬ on roads ●■●■●■●

Roads   major ▬▬▬▬   minor ▬▬▬▬

Selected other paths and side routes   ‒ ‒ ‒ ‒ ‒

Railways and stations ‒+++++++++●+++‒   buildings ▬

Field boundaries, where shown ‒‒‹‒   camp sites ⋏

Rivers ⇁⇁   streams ⇀   lakes, sea ◠

Boundaries of inset maps on 1:50,000 maps ‒ ‒‑ ‒

Trees   deciduous 🙠🙢   coniferous ↟ ↟   Summits ▲   churches, chapels +   youth hostels △

Scales - maps with numbers only - 1:50,000 (including 17A)
        maps with numbers and letters - 1:25,000 unless otherwise stated

North is at the top of the maps unless otherwise indicated

Mileage points ▬▬○   Electric power lines ⊼‒⌄‒⊼